Praise for *Other Tongues: psychologica*

'This is a courageous book that valu
within the therapeutic relationship.
world clinical examples, training and supervision, it stimulates
reflection on working with difference and identity. The practical
suggestions for working therapeutically with multilingualism are an
excellent resource for all therapists working in a multicultural world,
irrespective of theoretical orientation. This book is a major contribution
to the advancement of developing transcultural and cross-cultural
competencies in the therapeutic frame.'
**Divine Charura, Professor of Counselling Psychology, School of
Education, Language and Psychology, York St John University**

'*Other Tongues* focuses on the multilingual aspect of language in therapy,
exploring this through both a personal and political lens and teaching us
how multilingualism can be used as a therapeutic asset. Its examination
of how the themes of power, privilege and agency relate to language is
a timely and valuable contribution to the continuing dialogues in the
therapy field on systemic racism and anti-oppressive practice.'
**Jude Boyles, psychological therapist specialising in the refugee and
human rights field, manager of the Refugee Council's New Roots therapy
services in South Yorkshire, and editor of *Psychological Therapies for
Survivors of Torture* (PCCS Books, 2017)**

'Beverley's text provides a significant contribution to the area of
multilingualism within the field of psychological therapies. Despite our
rich multicultural and multiracial world, multilingualism has been a
rather neglected subject. It is now timely to grapple with what it means
to be bi/multilingual. Through this text, Beverley has opened up a
treasure box, illustrating the multifaceted and emotional meanings of
language. The text makes a strong argument that, in order to best serve
the needs of our clients, language and multilingualism matters *must be*
incorporated into therapeutic, interpreter and collegiate discussions.'
**Dr Zack Eleftheriadou, psychotherapist, Fellow of the British
Psychological Society, a British Psychoanalytic Council Scholar and
lecturer and pastoral tutor at the Institute of Arts in Therapy and
Education**

Other Tongues

Psychological therapies in a multilingual world

BEVERLEY COSTA

PCCS BOOKS

First published 2020

PCCS Books Ltd
Wyastone Business Park
Wyastone Leys
Monmouth
NP25 3SR
UK

Tel +44 (0)1600 891509
contact@pccs-books.co.uk
www.pccs-books.co.uk

Other Tongues: psychological therapies in a multilingual world

British Library Cataloguing in Publication Data.
A catalogue record for this book is available from the British Library

ISBN 978 1 910919 62 0

Cover design by Jason Anscomb
Printed in the UK by TJ International, Padstow

Dedication

To
ABCD
and
PQRS

About the author

Dr Beverley Costa grew up in East London in a family with three languages, two religions and two sets of cultural practices. After training as a counsellor, psychotherapist and group psychodramatist, she set up Mothertongue, a multi-ethnic counselling service, to meet a gap she observed in services for multilingual clients. In 2009 she created a pool of mental health interpreters within Mothertongue and in 2010 established the national Bilingual Therapist and Mental Health Interpreter Forum. Beverley founded The Pásalo Project in 2017 (www. pasaloproject.org) to disseminate learning from Mothertongue. She is a Senior Practitioner Fellow at Birkbeck, University of London, and has published a number of papers and chapters on therapy across languages. With Professor Jean Marc Dewaele, she won the 2013 BACP Equality and Diversity Research Award. Beverley has delivered training and supervision to statutory and voluntary sector health and social care organisations for the past two decades and has produced two anthologies of interpreters' stories and a play about a couple in a cross-language relationship, for the Soho Theatre, London. She co-founded the performance group of interpreters, *Around the Well*, in 2018.

Other Tongues:
psychological therapies in a multilingual world

Contents

	Foreword	*xi*
	Professor Suman Fernando	
	Introduction	*1*
1	Multilingualism, psychological therapies and the client perspective	8
2	Multilingualism and multilingual therapists	*31*
3	Interpreter-mediated therapy	*47*
4	Training to work with multilingualism in psychological therapies	*68*
5	Linguistically sensitive clinical supervision	*89*
6	Multilingualism in groupwork with children, adults and wider systems	*111*
	Conclusion	*121*
	Name index	*127*
	Subject index	*129*

Acknowledgements

Behind the pages and beyond the covers of this book are the work, courage and care of many people. A large number of those people were connected with Mothertongue – its outstanding team of counsellors, therapists, interpreters, group facilitators, volunteers, supervisors and managers. You will recognise aspects of your work and the experiences you have shared with me on every page. I am profoundly grateful to you. I would like to name every single one of you, but I know I don't need to. You know who you are.

It is a very sad fact that some of those who contributed with their commitment and their care are no longer with us. I was fortunate that I had the opportunity to learn from them while we had the time together. In this book, Tamara, your words of wisdom continue to live on.

Our clients at Mothertongue allowed us to learn alongside them. They were generous and tolerant with our clumsiness and they were excellent teachers. The same can also be said of Jean-Marc Dewaele – the extent of your open mind knows no bounds. Some of the counselling and interpreting teams also offered specific case material for me to include, and I would like to thank Ana Gaboleiro and Joanna Mungai for their thoughtfully descriptive accounts.

Writing this book hasn't come easily, and Catherine, you have smoothed the path and set me back on it with skill and with kindness. Phil, you have shown endless patience. You have read this book at least three times and you have looked after my every need while I was toiling away at it. Thank you.

Although you had already been born before the birth of Mothertongue, Sam and Rafe, it probably feels like it has been with you forever. You have grown up with it as the backdrop to our family life. Without your unfailing support, encouragement and holding me to account (including Dad, of course), I would not have found the courage, motivation and sense of fun I needed to live the experience and then to tell it.

My reluctance to write anything at all is linked to my relationship with English. Growing up with my Dad, I got used to his versions of idiomatic English expressions – 'Oh blooming hell. I think I am going around the corner [bend]'; 'I woke up this morning and I was feeling full of bones [beans].' It left me wondering for years if what I was talking in was actually a made-up language. Was it really the same language everyone else identified as English? But in the past few years I have come to embrace the weirdness of our home language. That's helped me, first to find the words, then to put those words in the right order, and last, to tell the story. The other factor that, beaver-like, nibbled away at my reluctance to write was my determination – more specifically, my determination to find a way to communicate the ideas that began with my family story and continued through the life of Mothertongue.

Doris Hordock and Costas Charalambous Pouyiouros, this book is because of you.

'I wonder if one can love, enjoy oneself [jouir], pray, die from pain or just die, plain and simple, in another language…'
Jacques Derrida[1]

'If you talk to a man in a language he understands, that goes to his head. If you talk to him in his language, that goes to his heart.'
Nelson Mandela[2]

1. Derrida J (1998). *Le Monolinguisme de l'Autre: ou la prothèse d'origine*. Paris: Editions Galilée (p2).

2. Widely attributed; pubished source not know.

Foreword

This is undoubtedly a book written by someone with a background of vast experience as a counsellor, psychotherapist and organiser of counselling services, plus study and deep thought about the complexities and joys of working cross-culturally with clients who are proficient and at ease in communicating in more than one language. In the discussions using examples from the field of counselling and psychotherapy, Beverley Costa demonstrates how language is not merely important for communication between client and therapist in a therapeutic setting but also tied up with how we all experience the world and make sense (or do not) of the nature and intensity of emotions we feel – matters that form the bread and butter of what we call psychology. At the same time, her book is full of practical advice for counsellors and other therapists. I reckon it should be read and studied by anyone who contemplates any sort of work in the field of psychological therapies, and particularly by counsellors and psychotherapists working in multicultural settings in the UK or any other similarly multicultural society. Such informative and thought-provoking books that are also practical guides are indeed few and far between.

In addition to its specialised nature, this book is a valuable addition to the general literature on socio-political aspects of mental health, especially in connection with issues of race and culture – matters that in the UK are largely to do with the struggle against racism. The book covers a wide field of topics, tracing how in each instance a sensitivity to multilingualism brings added value. They include the practice and teaching of psychological therapies, and especially counselling and psychotherapy; the teaching of these psychological skills, and organising and managing systems concerned with them; interpreter-mediated therapy, and group work with children and young people and adults. And in the course of all this, it covers topics such as personal identity, politics and social issues and the scientific study of linguistics, woven into the discussions and thence applied to have a very practical focus.

We often tend to think of language as just a means of communication, but this book demonstrates sharply that language plays a more complicated role when it is used in providing/receiving psychological therapies. For example, in the case of a multilingual client, the nature of the emotion(s) or feeling(s) they wish to talk about and understand in the course of therapy may require them to switch languages, and the author demonstrates the importance of enabling multilingual clients to do exactly this. This is something that may not be possible when communication between client and therapist is enabled by the use of an interpreter. The book demonstrates how the limitations caused by this problem can be circumvented and how the inclusion of an interpreter in the therapeutic conversation can provide the chance for deeper work to occur.

As well as its thoughtful understanding of the topics covered, this is a very practical book, written for practitioners, trainers, supervisors and managers engaged in delivering therapy to multilingual clients. Beverley Costa includes detailed descriptions of case histories and demonstrates practical ways in which the quality of therapy can be improved in what is broadly called transcultural or cross-cultural work. She tackles issues that may not be obvious to some people. There is guidance, for example, about how the limitations inherent in using an interpreter can be minimised and when it may be necessary to negotiate their role and function with the client and the interpreter.

Something that is just as important (for the reader of a book) is the expertise of the author in the field that they are writing about – in this instance, practical, down-to-earth work in psychological services – and the knack of the author to show the reader how it all works (or does not). Here are described in some detail therapeutic encounters where the nuances of language play a significant part in the success or otherwise of therapy. All in all, this comprehensive book is well worth careful reading and study and I recommend it to anyone working in the field of psychological therapies.

Professor Suman Fernando
Emeritus Professor of Social Sciences, London Metropolitan University
Formerly consultant psychiatrist, Enfield

Introduction

'Pass me the *schmutter* so I can give the *shissel* a bit of a clean.'
(English and Yiddish) – My mum to me in the kitchen.

'We'll go to the swimming pool tomorrow, *endaxi?*' (English and
Greek) – My dad to me in the garden.

Perhaps unsurprisingly, my interest in multilingualism,[1] multilingual
identities, linguistically embodied emotion and linguistically encoded
memories was born and nurtured during my early years, and it has
continued to develop ever since. I have become interested in people's
mother tongues and other tongues. Why do some people's tongues
hold more power than those of others? Sune Qvotrup Jensen (2011),
who explores the values associated with otherness, reminds us that:
'The other is always the other as in inferior, not as in fascinating'
(p65).

When I trained as a counsellor and psychotherapist in the 1990s,
I was surprised that this aspect of human experience did not feature
on the curriculum, especially when I remembered Nelson Mandela's
words about the languages of the head and the heart, quoted at the start
of the book. And it is not only the head/heart split that is implicated
linguistically. The psycholinguist Frank Smith (1992) claims that the
extent of people's understanding and agency in the world (the ability to
think, to make decisions and to act on them) varies according to their
linguistic capacity: 'One language sets you in a corridor for life. Two

---

1. A holistic approach to multilingualism defines all speakers with knowledge of more than
one language as multilingual (Dewaele, 2015).

languages open every door along the way.' Psychologists too are now acknowledging the place of bilingualism in developmental psychology (Byers-Heinlein et al, 2019).

Multilingual people are different from monolingual people

For counsellors and psychotherapists, this should surely be of interest, concerned as we are with people's perceptions of the world – from their perceptions of themselves and their sense of self-actualisation (Maslow, 1968) to their memories and emotions and the descriptions and construction and reconstruction of identities in narrative therapy (White & Epston, 1990). It seems that a client's sense of self is a core preoccupation in therapy. Clients' selves are constructed through the languages they speak:

> The language we speak influences not only the way we see the world around us, but also the way we see and think about ourselves – our self-perception, identity, autobiographical life narrative, in sum our self. (Marian & Kaushanskaya, 2004:198)

A few years after finishing my training, I was reminded again of the cost of ignoring people's languages when I heard a Turkish-speaking client talk about her experience of therapy in English (Telvi, 2006). To have therapy, to speak about her innermost feelings, felt like 'an arrow entering her body', she said. To hear her words spoken in a language that was not the language of her heart was a second arrow that pierced her. We may talk about the voice of the client in therapy, but where is the multilingual client's voice?

Multilingual clients are different from monolingual clients

I finished my counsellor and psychotherapy training in 2000, when I was living in Reading. Reading was, and is, a culturally and linguistically diverse town in England. Like many similar towns, there was some access to interpreters, but there was no counselling or therapeutic provision that took account of the particular, often complex needs of multilingual clients. And so I set up a charitable multi-ethnic counselling service called Mothertongue, which offered culturally and linguistically sensitive counselling and therapy to clients from the local black and minority ethnic communities, in their preferred languages. During its 18 years of service, Mothertongue won a number of awards for the quality of its therapeutic service and organisational structure and for its research. It was fully funded by a wide range of funders, meaning that all our psychotherapists and counsellors were employed as paid workers.

Our counsellors and psychotherapists were also all multilingual. We wanted to model how much we valued the multilingualism of our clients by having a multilingual workforce. We also wanted to be able to work directly with clients in their multiple languages without an interpreter, as well as with one.

Of course, we couldn't offer every one of the estimated 150 languages spoken in Reading (Get Reading, 2010) from within our own therapeutic workforce. So we also developed our own bank of mental health interpreters (again, all paid) and trained them to work collaboratively with the counsellors and psychotherapists. The mental health interpreters also provided interpreting support for mental health appointments with the local health trust, which paid us for this service.

These interpreters were all spoken-language interpreters. There may be overlaps with other professional areas – for example, sign language interpreting – but the experience of Mothertongue, and my own experience, is in the domain of spoken languages. The experiences of the Deaf community are not dealt with directly here, although I make reference to the important literature from that community in the chapters that deal with interpreting.

This book draws from Mothertongue's work between 2000 and 2018, when it closed. During that time, more than 3,000 clients received counselling, 4,000 interpreting appointments were offered and 1,000 people attended the group activities.

During Mothertongue's 18 years, a considerable amount of practice-based research was also produced. Most significantly, we established an award-winning research partnership with Jean-Marc Dewaele, Professor in Applied Linguistics and Multilingualism in the Department of Applied Linguistics and Communication at Birkbeck, University of London. This enabled a systematic exploration of the experience of multilingual counsellors, psychotherapists and clients, which is reported in the chapters that follow. The cross-disciplinary relationship between psychological therapies and applied linguistics provided us with ways of collaborating and learning about our familiar and unfamiliar working methods. This offered a parallel process for the subject matter we were investigating – people's experiences of themselves and of psychological therapy across familiar and unfamiliar languages.

The decision to close Mothertongue in 2018 was deliberate and planned and we prepared for it carefully over a period of two years. In the transition, a new organisation was formed called Pásalo (*www. pasaloproject.org* – it means 'Pass it on' in Spanish). The planned closure of Mothertongue was partly to enable us to embed some of our work into the local NHS mental health provision and partly to allow us to create a legacy of our learning and experience that we could pass on to others. This book is one of the ways in which we hope the legacy can be handed on.

While other authors have focused on the overall role of language in therapeutic dialogue, this book focuses on the multilingual aspect of language in psychological therapies. Chapter 1 looks at the experiences of multilingual clients and psychological therapies. Chapter 2 examines psychological therapies from the perspectives of multilingual counsellors and psychotherapists. Chapter 3 explores the challenges and opportunities offered by interpreter-mediated therapy and includes tips for working effectively in this way. Chapter 4 focuses on ways that training can prepare both monolingual and multilingual counsellors and psychotherapists to work with multilingualism as a therapeutic asset. Chapter 5 examines how linguistically sensitive supervision can build counsellors' and psychotherapists' confidence to work across languages with and without an interpreter. Chapter 6 considers how systemic thinking can incorporate multilingualism and includes examples of groupwork with children and adolescents, adults and wider social systems.

Six key themes run throughout the book and are covered in more than one chapter. I review the impact of people's multilingualism on the **identities** they hold in their different languages – someone can feel like an introvert in English and an extrovert in Arabic; someone else may find it impossible to get angry with an older person in Mandarin and yet find they enjoy shouting and complaining in Italian. I also consider how multilingualism is not only a personal issue, it is a **political** issue too. The languages we speak are a reflection of world histories of colonisation and there are intergenerational implications for the languages that we speak and those we do not speak. How aware are counsellors and psychotherapists of the prestige associated (or not) with the languages they use? I also consider how multilingualism impacts on ethical decision-making processes and how the languages spoken in the therapy room relate to three concepts that occupy the centre stage in psychological therapies: **power**, **privilege** and **agency**.

An additional theme connected with power is the counsellor or psychotherapist's anxiety about not understanding what is being said in the therapy room, where understanding and communication are the cornerstones of the work. I consider how, as counsellors and psychotherapists, we can increase our tolerance for not knowing and for dealing with our sense of **exclusion and inadequacy** that others' multilingualism can provoke in us. How do we amplify our awareness and reduce the extent of our unconscious bias – our socially-programmed people preferences, formed by our experiences and by our exposure to others' experiences of multilingualism? The theme of **multilingualism as an asset**, not a deficit, also recurs regularly throughout the book. I consider this alongside what is, perhaps, the book's central theme: that working with multilingualism in psychological therapies is not just a technical skill. It is not just a question of finding the right word for 'happy' in language X or Y, or 'being good at languages', or ensuring the interpreter speaks the same dialect as the client. Of course, technical issues are important because spoken language, as we will consider in Chapter 1, is central to talking therapists, as their title implies. But technical considerations often swamp the other more relational and process issues of multilingualism. It is easier to find solutions for the technical problems and think, 'That is the multilingual problem solved.' But, as we know, relational processes, which are at the heart of psychological therapies, are harder to address and to find solutions for.

The **technical v process** theme is embedded in all these five broad thematic areas. We will begin to look at this theme in the first chapter, where I explore how working with multilingualism in therapy requires more than technical considerations and skills. It is a complex process that needs careful attention and the adoption of a multilingual therapeutic frame of reference if it is to be used constructively in therapy.

This book is intended as a guide for professionals working in psychological therapies. It is not modality specific, and this is for a reason. Language forms the bedrock of all psychological models. The conceptual ideas about multilingualism presented in this book apply to all modalities when put into practice. Each chapter presents some of the issues, reviews research where appropriate, and then moves quickly into examples, drawing on real-world clinical, training and supervision scenarios. These scenarios are based on real experiences that have been anonymised, amalgamated and fictionalised to safeguard people's confidentiality. But the spirit of the clinical and training situations has been preserved, so that readers can immerse themselves into the material and imagine what they might do or not do in the moment if they were faced with a similar situation in practice.

I have tried to make myself sit with the unknown and tolerate the discomfort of feeling my way through a labyrinth of ideas, feelings and confusion in order to create the book I wanted to write. Over decades of working in this arena, I have absorbed experiences and become a particular shape (it happens to everyone, eventually). This means that, in order to communicate my ideas, I have had to deconstruct and extract myself from the bricolage so that I can rearrange and assemble the component parts into a shape that others can recognise and to which they can relate. On the way, I have stumbled, fallen and picked myself up again. If this book is useful and comes in a shape you can recognise as a guide, it is a tribute to the power of clumsiness and to falling over and getting up again. I hope that, as you read this book, you can also allow yourself to feel clumsy, try things out that you might not have done before and create your own shape, using the ideas I offer.

And a final note on terminology. In the book, I use the terms 'first language' to denote the first language or combination of languages a person learned when they were growing up, and 'home language(s)' for the language(s) spoken in a person's home when they were growing up. They may, or may not, be the same. 'Lingua franca' refers to the shared language that the practitioner and client choose to use, which may or may not be the first language of either. I also use the terms 'counsellor' and 'psychotherapist' either together or interchangeably, and sometimes just 'therapist'. This book is addressed to all those working in the psychological therapies professions – trainees, experienced practitioners, supervisors and trainers.

References

Byers-Heinlein K, Esposito AG, Winsler A, Marian V, Castro DC, Luk G (2019). The case for measuring and reporting bilingualism in developmental research. *Collabra: Psychology* 5(1): 37. https://doi.org/10.1525/collabra.233

Dewaele J-M (2015). Bilingualism and multilingualism. In: Tracy K, Ilie C, Sandel T (eds). *The International Encyclopedia of Language and Social Interaction*. Oxford: John Wiley & Sons (pp1-11).

Get Reading (2010). *150 different languages spoken in Reading schools*. [Online.] www. getreading.co.uk/news/local-news/150-different-languages-spoken-reading-4229840 (accessed 17 February 2018).

Jensen SQ (2011). Othering, identity formation and agency. *Qualitative Studies* 2(2): 63–78.

Marian V, Kaushanskaya M (2004). Self-construal and emotion in bicultural bilinguals. *Journal of Memory and Language* 51: 190–201.

Maslow AH (1968). *Toward a Psychology of Being*. New York, NY: Van Nostrand Reinhold Company.

Smith F (1992). *To Think: in language, learning and education*. London: Routledge.

Telvi J (2006). *Living in Translation: experiences of Turkish-speaking clients when they use interpreters*. Unpublished MA dissertation. London: Birkbeck, University of London.

White M, Epston D (1990). *Narrative Means to Therapeutic Ends*. New York, NY: WW Norton & Co.

1

Multilingualism, psychological therapies and the client perspective

'*Should you marry him?*' The question comes in English
'*Yes.*'
'*Should you marry him?*' The question echoes in Polish.
'*No…*'
'*Should you become a pianist?*' The question comes in English.
'*No, you mustn't. You can't.*'
'*Should you become a pianist?*' The question echoes in Polish.
'*Yes, you must. At all costs.*'
Hoffman (1989: 199)

A multilingual client is different from a monolingual client. But multilingualism is largely ignored in core therapy trainings, which tend to be rooted in a monolingual ideology. That is quite surprising, given that multilingualism is on the increase.[1] I have spent a long time wondering why this might be the case. Why would psychotherapists ignore a linguistic phenomenon when their profession is referred to as the 'talking cure'?

Possible explanations that have occurred to me cluster around the issue of power. They generally include anxieties about inclusion and exclusion – who understands and who doesn't; the poor reputation for

---

1. According to a 2018 European Commission survey, on average 80% of people aged 15–30 across all European Union member states can read and write in more than one language – although in the UK it is only 32%. https://data.europa.eu/euodp/en/data/dataset/S2186_466_ENG

and experiences of first-language English speakers when learning other languages, and the often unacknowledged colonial heritage and worldwide status of English as a prestige language and default lingua franca.

Another explanation, more specifically related to psychological therapies, is the recent emphasis placed on the embodied and somatic experiences of human beings. This attention to body language is very welcome in the treatment of, for example, trauma (Rothschild, 2000; van der Kolk, 2014).

This chapter focuses on the experiences of multilingual clients. Chapter 2 focuses on the experiences of multilingual therapists, and interpreter-mediated therapy is considered in Chapter 3.

In this chapter I will introduce the concepts of linguistic agency, privilege and empathy, linguistic attachment and loss. They may help to shed some light on the power issue I mentioned earlier. I will also consider findings from cross-disciplinary research with multilingual clients, with examples of case work to illustrate their practical application. The chapter concludes that attending to multilingualism can be a therapeutic asset in the treatment of trauma and other presenting issues and in the reduction of health inequalities.

I'll begin by looking at the need to pay attention to clients' multilingualism in therapy through a multilingual therapeutic frame.

The multilingual therapeutic frame

Psychological therapy is conducted within a therapeutic frame – the micro and the macro levels of structures that enable anxieties to be contained and worked with productively in mental health settings (Milner, 1952). The multilingual therapeutic frame introduces a linguistic perspective so that anxieties around language can be explored and contained actively, relationally and constructively in the clinical encounter – by clients and by practitioners in training and supervision.

Although multilingual clients are different from monolingual clients, most counselling and psychotherapy training models assume that their psychological presentations and treatment needs are the same. However, research has shown that most people *feel* different when they use different languages (Dewaele, 2016). People are also influenced by the topic of the conversation or speech (Panicacci & Dewaele, 2018). The extract that opens this chapter (Hoffman, 1989) demonstrates how you can feel and behave very differently in different languages. Hoffman's dilemma – whether to get married or to become a pianist – has different resolutions in the two languages she speaks.

Why is the multilingual experience important in counselling and psychotherapy? The multilingual population in the UK is increasing. For example, in 2010 in Reading, 150 languages were spoken in its schools (Get Reading, 2010). It is unlikely that this has decreased – according to more recent statistics, 35% of its primary school pupils and 26% of secondary school pupils did not speak English as their first language (Department for Education, 2016). The increase in multilingualism in the population will surely be reflected in the number of multilingual people seeking counselling and psychotherapy. Yet there is very little training for therapists and counsellors to equip them to work with multilingual clients.

Linguistic privilege

Power is a central dynamic in the counselling relationship (Proctor, 2017). We are living in an age of post-monolingualism, where the majority of people in the world are multilingual; how then do we justify behaving as if monolingualism were the norm (Yildiz, 2012)? Van Parijs (2004) describes this as linguistic injustice – the way in which some languages (such as English, which is currently the lingua franca of Europe) are dominant in discourses and have disproportionate power to influence (Komska, Moyd & Gramling, 2019), despite the huge racial and cultural diversity in societies today (Vertovec, 2007). It is very easy to continue this linguistic injustice in the therapy room, where people's other languages may be discounted or ignored because it is easier to work in a lingua franca. When a lingua franca is used, the multilingual client may be judged on how 'near-native' they sound.

This deficit model of multilingualism is challenged by some researchers, who prefer to view multilingualism as an asset (Dewaele, 2018). They use the term 'L1' instead of native language, as it is more neutral in tone. Others use the term 'home languages' to refer to the language spoken in someone's home environment when they are/were growing up.[2]

---

2. As previously noted in the introduction, in this book I use the terms 'first language' to denote the first language or combination of languages a person learned when they were growing up, and 'home language(s)' for the language(s) spoken in a person's home when they were growing up. 'Lingua franca' refers to the shared language that the practitioner and client choose to use, which may or not be the first language of either.

Monolingual, English-speaking therapists may not even think about the linguistic privilege they have in being able to speak one of the world's most powerful languages. A client who is trying to communicate in a language in which they do not feel confident may find it difficult to express sophisticated and complex thoughts and emotions. They may feel infantilised by the experience and that their sense of personal agency is diminished by their limited linguistic agency. De Maesschalck (2012) found that European migrants felt that healthcare providers underestimated the importance of language issues, which led to increased paranoia and aggression when they used health services. It seems that empathy for language difference, or linguistic empathy, is missing.

Linguistic empathy

Empathy is at the heart of the therapeutic endeavour. Carl Rogers defined empathy as a core condition for therapy. He described it as the 'sensitive ability and willingness to understand the client's thoughts, feelings, and struggles from the client's point of view' (1980: 85). It requires us to step out from our own experience of the world, reach across and take the perspective of another, while not losing our own sense of self. To achieve this, the therapist needs to be able to tune into their and their clients' cognitive processes and their emotional and embodied experiences (Elliott et al, 2011: Rogers, 1957). A therapist has to develop their capacity to dare to imagine different world views and experiences while assessing whether their imaginative constructions connect with their clients' realities. And, crucially, empathy involves therapists in getting to know themselves so that they do not mistake their own reactions for those of their clients. An empathic relationship with another requires us to have an empathic relationship with ourselves.

If we aim to live our lives in a way that is as egalitarian and non-oppressive as possible, it can be painful to acknowledge that, as first- language English speakers, we are privileged. We may not be aware of our linguistic privilege. The lack of status of some languages in comparison with English intersects with racialisation processes (Burck, 2005) and the legacy of colonisation. Therapists may strive to tolerate the guilt of their privilege because of race, class, educational achievement and so forth (Ryde, 2009; Eddo-Lodge, 2017) in order to avoid acting out their guilt/shame in the therapy room. But what about linguistic privilege? Do you perceive language as 'merely a vehicle' or as 'a barrier, never as a means to decolonise, or to experience the process'? (Phipps, 2019: 2). Unless we engage with the discomfort of our linguistic privilege, we will find it hard to be linguistically empathic. Empathy also involves the ability to tolerate ambiguity, misunderstanding and unfamiliarity with the terrain in another's world. These behaviours will be activated when we learn another language too. We have to shift out of a known structure, which includes grammar and vocabulary, into an unknown linguistic territory.

If we really want to understand a person who is speaking an unfamiliar language, we need to use our cognitive, imaginative, emotional and embodied experiences. Understanding that a client may be expressing different parts of themselves in different languages requires the sensitivity and openness to linguistic difference that I call 'linguistic empathy'. Understanding that a client may have a sense of their language as a low-status language requires us, as therapists, to engage with our own relationship with linguistic privilege. A linguistically empathic relationship with a client requires us to be familiar with our own relationships with the multiple aspects of multilingualism.

This will be illustrated in Dev's case, which we will consider in Chapter 5. Later in this chapter, we will also see how their linguistic empathy enabled the therapists working with Marc and Sarah to invite and welcome those different languages and emotional and embodied expressions into the therapeutic space. So, if we need to engage linguistic empathy and an understanding of linguistic privilege to work effectively with multilingual clients, where does an appreciation of multilingual agency fit in?

Linguistic agency and power

Language is at the centre of our ability to influence how we see the world (Sapir, 1958). It is also central to how we structure and give meaning to our experiences and form relationships with others, express our needs and feelings, conceptualise ideas and give shape to our imaginations. Language enables us not only to think but also to communicate our decisions, act and impact on others. This is what I mean by linguistic agency. The way in which language is used to communicate is a reflection of social and cultural norms, which help to regulate the individual and the community. The internal dialogue that starts this chapter illustrates with great clarity how splits in desires and values are carried by different languages.

Language is an essential component for helping us to form constructive relationships with people and also our relationships with ourselves and our sense of external reality. Felicity de Zulueta (2006) explains the evolutionary function of human language as providing the means whereby humans 'make sense of their external and internal world through increasingly complex conceptual representations'. She goes on to say:

> This creative interplay between human thought processes and environmental activities is what is referred to as 'culture': it is the product of a human mind in interaction with its environment. (2006: 329)

By naming feelings and experiences, we provide a frame for them. We give them a beginning and an end point. They are witnessed, they are acknowledged, and they can be survived.

A case example

Khin, a client from South East Asia, speaks in English in her counselling session about her sense of perfectionism, which is impeding her ability to finish her PhD in the UK. Khin maintains that there is no word for perfectionism in her home language, but she is aware that the drive does exist in her culture. By moving outside of her home culture and language, Khin is able to name the feeling and to think about the position she wants to adopt with regard to her sense of 'perfectionism'. Her second language and her new environment give her some mobility and choice. They give her a more dynamic, empowered and creative relationship with the drive she is experiencing (and has been experiencing for a long time). They also offer new ways for her to think about this drive and how she can act. Thus, her move to the UK and a new language give her a new type of linguistic agency. In this case, the use of English as the lingua franca in her counselling session is a liberating rather than a constraining factor. But the legacy of colonial languages is complex: for Khin, English has been a facilitator; for others it might be a constraint.

The way in which we use language to communicate offers us a model for making sense of how we feel and how we interact with and experience the world around us. Our use of language is one of the ways in which we can find a sense of agency in the world. When people have been traumatised by loss or violence, that sense of agency and connectedness to the outside world can be damaged. One's sense of identity is impacted. The language of pain is of interest not only to psychological therapists. The language embodiment (Pavlenko, 2012) of multilingual speakers, tested using electrodermal responses (Caldwell-Harris, 2014; Harris, Berko Gleason & Ayçiçeği, 2006), is of growing interest in applied linguistics too. However, attention to somatic experience and non-verbal communication in therapy and counselling has at times led to an unexamined belief that difficulties in linguistic communication can be overcome almost entirely by the use of and attention to body language. Such a view can ignore the agency that mastery in spoken language affords human beings.

Pain is language-destroying: '… (language) which would express and project the self is robbed of its source and its subject' (Scarry, 1985, quoted in Phipps, 2019: 20).

Our linguistic ability is one of the essential skills that helps human beings to move from a disempowered infancy to a productive and creative adulthood, or from a disempowered to an empowered adulthood where we can make choices and have influence – in other words, where we have agency. It helps us to make sense of our internal worlds and connect with the bigger reality outside of ourselves. It helps clients to make sense of early experiences and to integrate elements of the mind, body and soul.

And it is even more complex for multilinguals. Someone who stopped speaking their home language when they were a child or a young person may feel they have very little agency in that language as an adult. And, as we shall see in the following example, someone who was traumatised in one of their languages (whether or not it was their first language) may feel they no longer have a sense of agency when they are speaking that language. These are all issues that need to be attended to in therapy. Counsellors' and therapists' decisions to work or not to work therapeutically with clients' multilingualism could therefore be framed as an ethical issue.

A case example

Isabel is a counsellor working with Marc, a bilingual client – French is his first language, English his second. Marc has been living and working in England for a long time. For the past year, he has been bullied at work. The bullying has been so severe that he is now quite traumatised. Isabel and Marc use English as the lingua franca in the sessions, but Marc is so traumatised that he ends up feeling worse every time he tries to tell his story. Isabel, who does not speak French, invites Marc to tell the story in French and then back-translate it little by little into English so that she can understand. Marc is surprised to find that he does not feel so overwhelmed when he tells the story in French and that the cognitive act of translating it into English helps him to find a different, more empowered position in relation to the words.

Although Marc has a high enough level of linguistic agency to be able to get a job and to embark on counselling in English, the trauma of the workplace bullying has left him feeling like a disempowered infant when he uses it to revisit the trauma. Bessel van der Kolk (2000) reminds us that the retelling of a traumatic incident can be overwhelming for a client:

> Some patients, on recalling their trauma, may become flooded with both the traumatic memories and memories of previously forgotten traumas. (p19)

So, perhaps it should not be surprising that it is French, Marc's home language, that enables him to reconnect with a sense of agency and empowerment, as it is his non-traumatised language.

Marc still regularly uses French in his everyday life. But not everyone is in this position. If you do not have the opportunity (by choice or by circumstance) to speak your home language and you speak another language only partially, you may experience a sense of loss and inadequacy if you are unable to converse with eloquence. As I noted in the section on linguistic agency, this is often accompanied by a sense of infantilisation and of only being able to operate in society in a restricted and childlike way. In the words of a multilingual therapist:

> I have found that, when we are learning to speak another language, this touches that young part of ourselves – aged two or three. (Quoted in Costa, 2010: 20)

You may lose not only your linguistic agency but also your fluency in your home language over time – an experience known as 'language attrition' (Schmid, 2013). Language attrition can be experienced as painful or longed for (a new language can represent a possible escape route), or it may be hardly noticed. Language attrition may bring with it other socio-psychological functions attributable to the new languages. Speaking additional languages may evoke not only feelings of loss at not being able to use one's native language but also a sense of gain – for example, ability to speak other languages can increase our range of expression. In the following section, we will consider the gains as well as the losses associated with speaking new languages.

Linguistic attachment and loss

For multilingual clients, there is a deeply important psychological attachment that is not explained by any of the traditional models of counselling and psychotherapy. People have an attachment (positive or negative) to their languages and to the contexts in which they are learned and used (Amati-Mehler, 1993; de Zulueta, 1995; Hammer, 2016; Pérez Foster, 1998; Tehrani & Vaughan, 2009). Later in the chapter, we will see how early audio attachments impact on children's sense of safety and belonging when choosing friends.

Sometimes, as indicated in the previous section, people may view the opportunity to learn a new language as a means of moving away from their past and creating a new future. But this is not the case for everyone, and it depends on the context. As we saw with Marc, it was his 'old' language, French, that helped him move beyond the trauma.

Sometimes people have such a strong attachment to their home language and such a fear of losing it that they are unable to learn another language. Their language may be their last tie to home and adding another may feel like a betrayal. The title of Lily Wong Fillmore's paper (1991) hints at such an experience: 'When learning a second language means losing the first.'

This does not come as a surprise when you think that our first language frequently has a heightened emotionality in comparison with an additional language, due to several factors: the family context of learning; that first-language learning co-evolves with the development of emotional regulation systems, and that first languages have greater connections with subcortical brain structures that mediate arousal (including amygdala-mediated learning) (Caldwell-Harris, 2014). In the early years, acquisition of the first language can be understood in attachment terms as the main way in which the infant begins to separate from the mother (Winnicott, 1971), as well as the means to relate to others (Stern, 1998). The relationship the child has to their acquisition of language and the experience of separation are therefore inextricably linked. In later life, some people may lose their home language, actively or passively (Schmid, 2013). Others find it very difficult to acquire a new language when they migrate. This may be because learning the new language excites anxieties around separation and loss – not only of the mother but also of the mother tongue and the motherland.

Below are the words of a 17-year-old refugee from Afghanistan describing his experience of forced migration and the losses, including that of his first language:

> It is very hard for a person who leaves everything, his country,
> language, food, clothes, people and family. We know that
> if they haven't got problems, they would never leave them
> because these things can be loved once ever in their life. But
> unfortunately, they have to, to save their life and live calmly.

Which language for therapy and counselling?

So, should it be the first language or other languages for therapy? The traditional view is that therapeutic work is best conducted in the client's first language (Fernando, 2003). Pérez Foster wonders if, when she conducts therapy with clients in English as a lingua franca, she is actually conducting therapy at all. She uses the terms 'pseudotherapy' and 'quasitherapy' to draw our attention to the dilemma surrounding language choice in therapy. She questions:

> … whether our English work is a 'pseudotherapy' which simply
> sides with the patient's resistance to the mother tongue and the
> mother era, or a 'quasitherapy' where the essential material is lost
> in the complex cognitive traffic of bilingualism and its ensuing
> impact on translation. (1998: 202)

Sue and Sue (1999), echoing the comments earlier in the chapter about the use of a lingua franca, make the point that the use of English as the standard means of communication immediately disadvantages those unable to communicate fluently in English. Some clients may find it a comfort to be able to speak in their home language (Gilbert, 2005). And we may only be able to access some emotions experienced in early childhood in the languages we spoke at that time. But working with multilingualism in therapy requires more than technical considerations and skills. Not all multilinguals have the same linguistic profiles and needs. Moving between languages is a complex process that needs to be understood if it is to be used in therapy. For the multilingual person, it can sometimes be a therapeutic choice to speak in a latterly acquired language. Some emotions may be accessible to the multilingual person in one of their languages and not in others. It depends on when and how the languages have been learned (Dewaele, 2018). Languages learned in later life can circumvent the constraining adult voices from our childhoods. We hear those voices in the languages in which those adults spoke to us. A different language can permit the expression of emotions that may have been discouraged when we were growing up. And, as mentioned, some people may lose their first language, by choice or by accident, and this language attrition can have an unexpected psychological impact.

Research into multilingualism in therapy

There is a growing body of research that shows that the choice of language in therapy is far more complex than the 'first language good, other languages bad' formula. A cross-disciplinary and cross-professional approach has been helpful to deepen the understanding of the role of multilingualism in therapy across both applied linguistics and psychotherapy. It has been useful to examine multilingualism through different academic and cultural lenses. The findings from this research (Costa & Dewaele, 2012; Dewaele & Costa, 2013; Rolland, Dewaele & Costa, 2017) are reported fully elsewhere and I will only summarise them here.

A three-phase model, using observation, analysis and implementation, framed the formal research that underpins the rest of this chapter. The three phases comprised, first, the initial formal research; second, the application of the findings to the training programme design and delivery, and third, the evaluation of the impact of training programmes. I will consider the second two phases, which address training and clinical supervision for multilingual therapy, in later chapters.

The results from the first phase of the cross-disciplinary research suggest that speaking an additional language can serve a number of sociopsychological functions: identity formation and sense of belonging; access to or blocking of early memories; expression of emotions, and recovery from traumatic experiences. These functions can be held in mind within the multilingual therapeutic frame when we work with distress and coping across languages.

Identity-formation and sense of belonging

The ways in which people's identities are formed and their sense of self is developed are linked to the languages they have learned and choose to speak. Language is intrinsically linked with our sense of identity (Pavlenko, 2005, 2014). People who speak more than one language frequently report that they feel that aspects of their identity and personality are expressed or suppressed differently in different languages (Dewaele, 2016). When they speak in only one of their languages, they may feel that they are representing only a part of themselves.

For people who are multilingual, the way in which experiences and emotional reactions are encoded becomes more complex when more than one language is spoken. One of the ways in which multilinguals cope is by creating new selves for each of the languages spoken (Panicacci & Dewaele, 2017). Louise Rolland suggests that these differences in linguistic selves encompass personality traits, roles and responsibilities and the ability to express emotions:

> While this multiplicity can be a source of confusion and conflict, particularly when one language and culture have been minoritised, many examples point to multilinguals' creative use of their linguistic repertoire to perform and reinvent themselves in different contexts. (Rolland, 2019: 30)

Priska Imberti (2007), who migrated from Argentina to New York as a young woman, refers to the new self she had to create: one that reflected an inner connectedness with the new culture. People who are multilingual deal with the tensions of plural identities in varying ways. Some find they feel they do not belong anywhere. Others revel in the sense of belonging in more than one context:

> … I do not feel impaired, I just adapt, which is what I learned to do while travelling and living in all the countries I know.
> (Therapist quoted in Costa, 2010: 21)

Memory recall and expression of emotion

The potential to move between languages can enhance memory recall, as autobiographical experiments have confirmed (Schrauf, 2000). Childhood memories are found to be richer and more emotionally charged in therapy when recounted in the first language (Dewaele & Costa, 2013):

> ... when I mixed in some words from my [first language], it started to make more sense talking about my childhood... I just needed some key words in my [first language] to bring memories back. (2013: 13)

Speaking in a latterly acquired language can also enable a fresh expression of emotions that a first language inhibits. Maybe as a child, the expression of anger or swearing were discouraged. People report that they are surprised to find they are more disinhibited in another language (Dewaele, 2013), although, according to Harris and colleagues (2006), it is not the earlier acquired language but the language in which they are most proficient that carries and expresses more emotion. The following case example illustrates the way in which moving between languages can elicit different levels of emotional intensity, linguistic agency and recall.

A case example

Eva, a therapist, speaks a range of languages fluently. Spanish is her first language, followed by French, English and Brazilian Portuguese. She works as a therapist in all her languages. Her client Sarah's first language is Czech. She has lived for many years in the UK and has a Brazilian partner – a long-term relationship in which English is the lingua franca. She says that she only functions in English now.

Sarah's mother died three months before Sarah came for therapy. Sarah feels she was never good enough for her mother and has been left with complex feelings of grief and anger towards her. During therapy, it becomes clear that Sarah wants to be able to address her grief. Eva suggests empty-chair work and asks Sarah to bring a photo of her mother so that they can make the empty chair feel more real. Sarah agrees to try.

Sarah brings the photo to the next session. She is quite dismissive about it. But when it comes to the empty-chair exercise, she freezes. Eva gently 'nudges her' to put the photo on the chair. Sarah does this but is still unable to speak. Eva nudges her again by saying she will say the words for her initially, so that Sarah will not have to start from cold. Sarah is deeply touched by Eva's nudging. She says this has made her feel that Eva truly cares and that this is what inspired her to trust her over the weeks. Eva explains that she will speak in English and that Sarah can translate her words into Czech, as this was the language in which she spoke with her mother.

At this point Eva is thinking that she will build a scaffold for Sarah to begin to speak Czech again, first through the act of translating – (ie. carrying out a technical, cognitive task and not having to think creatively of what to say to her mother). Sarah says again that she cannot speak Czech anymore; that she has forgotten it completely, she only speaks English and she can say things better in English. Eva replies: 'But you only spoke to your mother in Czech, didn't you?' At this point, Sarah agrees to have a go at the translation.

The attempt is successful. Sarah manages to translate and, with Eva's encouragement, she is then able to express her own feelings to her mother in her own way and in her own words, with a great deal of emotion. She cries in a way that she was unable to do at her mother's funeral.

Eva's linguistic empathy significantly contributes to the successful outcome. Eva introduces the idea of bringing in Sarah's different languages. She even gives Sarah the role of translator, so that she can approach the intensity of her home language in a more cognitively detached way. By working within a multilingual therapeutic frame, Eva is able to use Sarah's linguistic history and her relationship to her languages, and to Eva, as therapeutic assets.

Recovery from traumatic experiences

We have already seen that language can serve many functions for us. It has the capacity to sooth us and it can offer us protection. Paul Gilbert (2005) suggests that the self-soothing neuropathway, which needs to be activated in order for healing to progress, is developed in childhood and is often associated with the first language. For example, in therapy a client may find it helpful to try out relaxation techniques in their home language. But it is important to understand some of the client's linguistic history. The home language may not always be the most soothing language. Traumatised clients will have encoded the traumatic experience in the language in which it has been experienced. Tehrani and Vaughan (2009) propose that the use of bilingual differences and language switching in therapy can increase emotional mastery, as we saw in Marc's case earlier in the chapter. He was better able to speak in French about being bullied in English without feeling overwhelmed. Tehrani and Vaughan assert that the language in which the trauma is experienced – whether it is a first, second or subsequent language – is the language that will carry the emotional charge for this incident. If the trauma was experienced in the childhood language, the subsequent languages may be able to provide the soothing. Additional languages may be used for protection and first languages for expression, or vice versa, depending on the context. Bessel van der Kolk (2000) proposes that it may be necessary for a person to gain some emotional distance from the traumatic incident in order to be able even to talk about it:

> In order to help traumatized individuals process their traumatic memories, it is critical that they gain enough distance from their sensory imprints and trauma-related emotions so that they can observe and analyze these sensations and emotions without becoming hyperaroused or engaging in avoidance manoeuvers. (p18)

People are likely to make more utilitarian choices when they use a foreign language instead of their first or home language (Costa, 2020). So, using a different language from the 'traumatised language' can provide cognitive distance and emotional detachment (Pavlenko, 2012) until the client is ready to tolerate the intensity of feelings.

And we have also seen how Marc's act of translation, back into the 'traumatised (more emotionally charged) language', can start to de-toxify that language. The cognitive act of translation can decode and decrease the intensity of the traumatic current of the traumatised language. This can be a helpful technique to move the client along their therapeutic journey, as we saw with the example of Sarah. She was only able to access her emotional response to her mother's death in her first language, even though she claimed to have completely lost it – her 'mother tongue'.

In our experience at Mothertongue, a refugee client who is a survivor of torture might want to speak only in her newly acquired English in order to establish distance between herself and her torturer, who shared her home language. Another Mothertongue client taught his counsellor a few words, including the word for 'stop', in his home language. He wanted to hear the counsellor say it if his anxiety levels became raised significantly during a breathing exercise.

Conversely, the second or subsequent language can be the most facilitative language for a client in counselling and therapy. The following case example illustrates how a client found a voice for herself (which she never had in her first language) in her newly acquired language.

A case example

Nina, a counsellor, has been seeing her Farsi-speaking client, Yasmin, for five sessions, with the help of an interpreter. The interpreter does not turn up for the sixth session, so Nina and Yasmin agree to continue the session in English. Nina is surprised at how easily they can communicate. She is even more surprised that Yasmin tentatively starts to speak for herself. From that day on, they work without an interpreter and Yasmin's confidence steadily begins to build. In English, Yasmin is able to find a new sense of agency and to allow herself to express her needs in a way that she never could in her native Farsi.

It can be just by chance that a therapist discovers the power of speaking with a client in a lingua franca. The example of Yasmin is a useful reminder that there is no easy formula about which language will be most therapeutic. A client's linguistic history can provide clues as to which languages can be most useful in different contexts. I will discuss how to take a client's linguistic history at the end of the chapter.

Sarah's last session with Eva illustrates the way in which languages can have the capacity to soothe and heal and also how first languages can give voice to the expression of deep feelings of loss and attachment. Moving between languages can help people to process traumatic and other difficult experiences, such as bereavement, and provide that sense of emotional mastery to which Tehrani and Vaughan (2009) refer.

At the final session, Sarah again brings the photo of her mother. This time, she has framed it, and she holds it close to her heart. She says that during the week she has been 'talking' to her mother in Czech and that she is feeling much lighter and nearer to being able to let her go and feel at peace with her. She is shocked and amazed that she has been able to reconnect with the Czech language, that she has been able to find another position through the different languages and that it has had such a powerful effect.

Sarah is shocked to find she has not, as she had thought, totally forgotten her first language. However, research suggests that an early language that is spoken until about 12 years of age will be fairly resistant to erosion; even if you migrate, it is unlikely that you will truly forget your mother tongue (Schmid, 2011). Language switching facilitated the process of Sarah's reconnection and reattachment to her mother tongue. But the technical process of language switching would not have occurred without the relational process, within the multilingual therapeutic frame, of the therapist's linguistic empathy.

A note on language-switching in therapy

Switching between different languages is known as code-switching and is a communicative function of multilingualism (Gardner-Chloros, 2009). It refers to the way multilingual people use elements of more than one language within a conversation. Analysing how and why people choose to switch languages can reveal how it is used to manage emotional expression and the intensity of feelings. Dewaele (2013) suggests that people may find it easier to express anger in a latterly acquired language because they hear their own words with less weight and less impact. Conversely, Sarah was only able to really feel her loss when she spoke in Czech, the language in which she had conducted her relationship with her mother.

The choice of language at any given time can be a useful tool in understanding someone's anxieties and coping strategies. But, in the words of a colleague, Maud Muscat, visiting lecturer in counselling for young people at the University of Malta: 'At times, it is just a word' (Muscat, personal communication).

In my research with Jean-Marc Dewaele (2012, 2013), we explored how code-switching could be used in counselling and therapy as a therapeutic asset in terms of the therapist's perceived attunement and the client's ability to approach (immerse themselves in its expression) or distance (protect) themselves from strong emotion. It did not seem to matter to many multilingual clients if their therapist spoke and understood their other languages. The most crucial factor for clients was the therapist's linguistic empathy. This was demonstrated by the therapist or counsellor's willingness to engage with their client's multilingualism, whether by being comfortable with code-switching or being able to tolerate not immediately understanding and/or waiting for the client to back-translate what they had said. Some clients reported that they felt a therapist stepped into their world when they were invited to bring their other language(s) into the room at an appropriate moment: 'It felt she wanted that part of me not to be neglected or suppressed' (Rolland, Dewaele & Costa, 2017: 12).

Practical suggestions for working therapeutically with multilingualism

It can be useful to think about what language proficiency and linguistic agency mean to your client. Perez Foster (1998) encourages counsellors and psychotherapists to take a linguistic history as part of the assessment process.

These questions may be useful initial prompts in an assessment session with clients:

- What have your experiences of learning a new language been like?

- How old do you feel in your different languages?

- What does proficiency in the language represent for you?

- What do you think you might gain from achieving proficiency in the new language?

- What might you lose in the process of becoming proficient in a new language?

- In which language do you find it easier to get angry/express affection/be professional?

- Which language(s) do you dream in?

- Do you speak in specific languages with specific people?

- What prompts you to code-switch?

Linguistic empathy opens the practitioner to an awareness of how language is used in the room. For example, is more than one language used? If so, why and when? Can you tolerate not understanding what is being said for a short while? Can you think of ways to invite clients' languages into the room safely, even if you don't understand them? What does language switching enact in the therapy? Is a language ignored or prioritised in the therapeutic work and, if so, why? Who is making the most linguistic effort in the room? Do you acknowledge that your client may be making all the effort linguistically to converse in a foreign language while you are speaking in your first language? You might ask your client how they feel talking to you in each of their languages.

You may find that you begin to think more about ways to simplify and demystify your language. You might consider issues of power and linguistic privilege in your communication. Perhaps you speak the language used in the therapy better or worse than your client. What is that like? Do you share a language with your client because of a shared colonial history – are you speaking a colonial lingua franca? Research conducted with children aged five and six years old (Paquette-Smith et al, 2019) found that they tended to choose their friends by how they spoke (shared accent and vocabulary etc) rather than by their physical appearance. This is not surprising, given that our earliest attachments are formed in the womb and then with our primary caregivers whose voices we hear around us as we grow through our early, formative years. What is the way you speak saying about you and your client, and how is that addressed in the counselling room? In couples therapy where the couple speak different languages, which of a couple's languages are used in the room and which are excluded?

You might like to learn a language, or recall your experience of trying to learn a language , and reflect on its impact on, for example, your sense of identity, your self-esteem, your understanding of others and your sense of agency.

Conclusion

This chapter has considered the experiences and therapeutic needs of multilingual clients, including the concepts of linguistic agency, privilege and empathy; linguistic attachment and loss, and the practical application of findings from cross-disciplinary research with multilingual clients. A client's multilingualism can be a therapeutic asset. Choosing whether to attend to or ignore a client's multilingualism is therefore an ethical issue. Dewaele (2013) quotes a language teacher's comments on the lack of confidence that we in Britain have about learning languages:

> I think that people still view learning other languages with a
> sense of fear. There seems to be this mystique about learning

languages and many people decide early on in their lives that they can't do it. (Dewaele, 2013: 262).

As practising counsellors and psychotherapists, we need to overcome this fear if we are to provide a truly accessible and high-quality service to clients who use other languages. Health inequalities cannot be reduced just by improving access. The quality and the courage of the therapeutic work is essential to the outcomes. Through preparation and exposing ourselves to another language (either by learning a new language and/or by becoming more familiar with the nuances and irregularities of our own language), therapists can become more empathic, less fearful and more effective in working with clients who do not share their first language. Alison Phipps reminds us that taking clients' multilingualism seriously in the therapeutic process is a difficult but necessary task, particularly in the context of colonialism:

> Something substantial has to be risked, some threshold has to be crossed into something which is not knowable, until one is over on the other side... for decolonising to happen, however temporary it may be...' (Phipps, 2019: 28)

The multilingual therapeutic frame can help to contain the anxieties that arise when crossing that linguistic threshold. In the next chapter, I will consider the experiences and needs of multilingual therapists.

References

Amati-Mehler J, Argentario S, Canestri J (1993). *The Babel of the Unconscious: mother tongue and foreign tradition*. Madison, CT: International Universities Press.

Burck C (2005). *Multilingual Living: explorations of language and subjectivity*. London: Palgrave Macmillan.

Caldwell-Harris CL (2014). Emotionality differences between a native and foreign language: implications for context-dependence and embodiment. *Frontiers in Psychology: Language Sciences*; 30 March. https://bu.academia.edu/CatherineCaldwellHarris/

Costa A (2020). *The Bilingual Brain and What it Tells Us about the Science of Language*. New York, NY: Penguin Random House, 2020.

Costa B (2010). Mother tongue or non-native language? Learning from conversations with bilingual/multilingual therapists about working with clients who do not share their native language. *Journal of Ethnicity and Inequalities in Health and Social Care* 3(1): 15–24.

Costa B, Dewaele J-M (2012). Psychotherapy across languages: beliefs, attitudes and practices of monolingual and multilingual therapists with their multilingual patients. *Language and Psychoanalysis 1*: 19–41 (reprinted in *Counselling and Psychotherapy Research 2014; 14*(3): 235–244).

De Maesschalck S (2012). *Linguistic and Cultural Diversity in The Consulting Room: a tango between physicians and their ethnic minority patients.* (Unpublished Doctoral dissertation). Ghent: Ghent University.

Department for Education (2016). *Schools, Pupils and their Characteristics: January 2016.*[Online.]www.gov.uk/government/statistics/schools-pupils-and-their-characteristics-january-2016 (accessed 16 June 2020).

De Zulueta F (2006). *From Pain to Violence: the traumatic roots of destructiveness* (2nd ed). Ontario: John Wiley & Sons.

De Zulueta F (1995). Bilingualism, culture and identity. *Group Analysis 28*: 179–190.

Dewaele J-M (2018). Why the dichotomy 'L1 versus LX user' is better than 'native versus non-native speaker'. *Applied Linguistics 39*(2): 236–240.

Dewaele J-M (2016). Why do so many bi- and multilinguals feel different when switching languages? *International Journal of Multilingualism 13*: 92–105.

Dewaele J-M (2013). *Emotions in Multiple Languages* (2nd ed). Basingstoke: Palgrave Macmillan.

Dewaele J-M, Costa B (2013). Multilingual clients' experience of psychotherapy. *Language and Psychoanalysis 2*(2): 31–50.

Eddo-Lodge R (2017). *Why I'm No Longer Talking to White People About Race.* London: Bloomsbury Publishing.

Elliott R, Bohart AC, Watson JC, Greenberg LS (2011). Empathy. In: Norcross J (ed). *Psychotherapy Relationships that Work* (2nd ed). New York, NY: Oxford University Press (pp132–152).

Fernando S (2003). *Cultural Diversity, Mental Health and Psychiatry.* Hove: Brunner-Routledge.

Fillmore LW (1991). When learning a second language means losing the first. *Early Childhood Research Quarterly 6*(3): 323–346.

Gardner-Chloros P (2009). *Code-switching.* Cambridge: Cambridge University Press.

Get Reading (2010). *150 different languages spoken in Reading schools.* [Online.] www.getreading.co.uk/news/local-news/150-different-languages-spoken-reading-4229840 (accessed 17 February 2018).

Gilbert P (2005). *Compassion: conceptualisations, research and use in psychotherapy.* London: Routledge.

Hammer K (2016). Bilingual bonds: acculturation, attachment, and being yourself in a new language. *International Journal of Language and Culture 3*(2): 253–279.

Harris CL, Berko Gleason J, Ayçiçeği A (2006). When is a first language more emotional? Psychophysiological evidence from bilingual speakers. In: Pavlenko A (ed). *Bilingual Minds*. Bristol: Multilingual Matters Ltd (pp257–283).

Hoffman E (1989). *Lost in Translation: a life in a new language*. Heinemann: London.

Imberti P (2007). Who resides behind the words? Exploring and understanding the language experience of the non-English-speaking immigrant. *Families in Society: the journal of contemporary social services 88*(1):67-73.

Komska Y, Moyd M, Gramling D (2019). *Linguistic Disobedience: restoring power to civic language*. London: Palgrave Macmillan.

Milner M (1952). Aspects of symbolism in comprehension of the not-self. *International Journal of Psychoanalysis 33*: 181–195.

Panicacci A, Dewaele J-M (2018). Do interlocutors or conversation topics affect migrants' sense of feeling different when switching languages? *Journal of Multilingual and Multicultural Development 39*(3): 240–255.

Panicacci A. Dewaele J-M (2017). 'A voice from elsewhere': migration, personality and multiple selves in multiple languages. *International Journal of Multilingualism 14*(4): 419–436.

Paquette-Smith M, Buckler H, White KS, Choi J, Johnson EK (2019). The effect of accent exposure on children's sociolinguistic evaluation of peers. *Developmental Psychology 55*(4): 809–822.

Pavlenko A (2014). *The Bilingual Mind: and what it tells us about language and thought*. Cambridge: Cambridge University Press.

Pavlenko A (2012). Affective processing in bilingual speakers: disembodied cognition? *International Journal of Psychology 47*(6): 405–428.

Pavlenko A (2005). *Emotions and Multilingualism*. Cambridge, MA: Cambridge University Press.

Pérez Foster R (1998). *The Power of Language in the Clinical Process: assessing and treating the bilingual person*. Northvale, NJ: Aronson.

Phipps A (2019). *Decolonising Multilingualism: struggles to decreate*. Bristol: Multilingual Matters.

Proctor G (2017). *The Dynamics of Power in Counselling and Psychotherapy: ethics, politics and practice* (2nd ed). Monmouth: PCCS Books.

Rogers CR (1980). *A Way of Being*. Boston, MA: Houghton Mifflin.

Rogers CR (1957). The necessary and sufficient conditions of therapeutic personality change. *Journal of Consulting Psychology 21*: 95–103.

Rolland L (2019). *Multilingual selves in psychotherapy: a mixed methods study of multilingual clients' experiences and language practices*. Thesis submitted for the degree of Doctor of Philosophy Applied Linguistics and Communication. London: Birkbeck, University of London.

Rolland L, Dewaele J-M, Costa B (2017). Multilingualism and psychotherapy: exploring multilingual clients' experiences of language practices in psychotherapy. *International Journal of Multilingualism* 14(1): 69–85.

Rothschild B (2000). *The Body Remembers: the psychophysiology of trauma and trauma treatment*. New York, NY: WW Norton.

Ryde J (2009). *White identity in psychotherapy: can dialogic, intersubjective psychotherapy help white people work more effectively in a racialized context?* Marianne Fry Lecture, Bristol. https://mariannefrylectures.uk/past-lectures/ (accessed 15 June 2020).

Sapir E (1958). *Culture, Language and Personality.* Berkeley, CA: University of California Press.

Scarry E (1985). *The Body in Pain: the making and unmaking of the world.* Oxford: Oxford University Press.

Schmid MS (2013). First language attrition. *WIREs Cognitive Science* 4(2): 117–123.

Schmid MS (2011). *Language Attrition.* Cambridge: Cambridge University Press.

Schrauf RW (2000). Bilingual autobiographical memory: experimental studies and clinical cases. *Culture and Psychology* 6: 387–417.

Stern D (1998). *The Interpersonal World of the Infant.* London: Karnac.

Sue DW, Sue D (1999). *Counselling the Culturally Different: theory and practice* (3rd ed). New York, NY: John Wiley & Sons.

Tehrani N, Vaughan S (2009). Lost in translation: using bilingual differences to increase emotional mastery following bullying. *Counselling and Psychotherapy* 9(1): 11–17.

van der Kolk BA (2014). *The Body Keeps the Score: brain, mind, and body in the healing of trauma.* New York, NY: Viking.

van der Kolk BA (2000). Posttraumatic stress disorder and the nature of trauma. *Dialogues in Clinical Neuroscience* 2(1): 7–22.

Van Parijs P (2004). Europe's linguistic challenge. *European Journal of Sociology* 45(01): 113–154.

Vertovec S (2007). Super-diversity and its Implications. *Ethnic and Racial Studies* 30(6): 1024–1054.

Winnicott DW (1971). *Playing and Reality.* London: Tavistock Publications Ltd.

Yildiz Y (2012). *Beyond the Mother Tongue: the postmonolingual condition.* New York, NY: Fordham University Press.

2

Multilingualism and multilingual therapists

'I feel like a fraud.'

Multilingual therapists can feel their therapeutic skills melting away when they start to practise in their home languages (Costa & Dewaele, 2012; Verdinelli & Biever, 2009). When a counsellor/therapist embarks on training, we create a new professional identity for ourselves that uses the language in which we train. This chapter will outline the challenges that face multilingual therapists when working with multilingual clients. I will argue that multilingual therapists need to find a professional identity that uses all the languages in which they intend to practise.

As we have already seen, a multilingual therapist's decision to work across languages is not just about technique; it is far more complex. However, if they have never worked multilingually, the multilingual therapists I have spoken to often see it as a purely technical choice. The main challenge they raise is that there is no equivalence between one language and another (Apresjan, 1974). And, of course, it is true that some concepts are particularly hard to translate. How do you translate, for instance, the yearning expressed in 'Quem me dera?' in the original Portuguese, or capture the nuances that the German word 'Gratwanderung' expresses – a word that means 'walking along mountain ridges' but was eloquently translated by one of my research participants as 'the narrow zone that humans inhabit'?

And the professional identity does not translate automatically either. Priska Imberti, a psychotherapist originally from Argentina and now working in the US, argues that we create a new identity when we learn a new language – one that is connected to that language's culture:

> When we change languages, both our worldview and our identities get transformed. We need to become new selves to speak a language that does not come from our core self, a language that does not reflect our inner-connectedness with the culture it represents. (Imberti, 2007: 71)

Findings from the psychophysiological research on multilingual experiences mentioned in the previous chapter (Caldwell-Harris, 2014) seem to indicate that languages are embodied differently (Pavlenko, 2012), depending on the person's age and the learning context. Experiments with multilingual participants (Caldwell-Harris, 2014) have shown that there is heightened electrodermal reactivity when the participants listen to emotionally charged words in their first languages. At Mothertongue, clients told us that they held and felt their languages in different parts of their bodies.

Other authors (Shaw, 2003; Totton, 2015) have explored the embodied identity of the psychotherapist more generally. I would extend this to suggest that psychotherapists (and clients) embody their cultural and professional identities differently in their different languages. I propose that it is the process rather than the technicalities of working multilingually and the relational implications of the multilingual encounter that are often the hardest challenges for multilingual therapists. In the following sections, I will explore what experienced multilingual therapists have to say about these challenges and then look more specifically at issues of professional identity, over-identification, collusion and avoidance. I will end with a case illustration.

Multilingual therapists' experiences

A range of studies (Biever et al, 2002; Costa, 2010; Costa & Dewaele, 2012; Nguyen, 2014) report that multilingual therapists can feel unsupported, unacknowledged and unprepared for working across languages. Too often, service managers ask multilingual therapists to work in their first or home language, even if they did not train in that language and do not use it in their own counselling, therapy or supervision. It is assumed that it is easy, or even easier, for a therapist to work in their first language, regardless of the language in which they trained.

In 2010 I conducted some small-scale research with six experienced multilingual counsellors, none of whom were native English speakers, about their experiences with multilingual clients (Costa, 2010). Several themes emerged from the replies to the survey questionnaires. The counsellors talked about the losses involved in not speaking your native tongue, and of learning to live in a new culture. But most felt that their own multilingualism was relevant and important to the positive outcome of the counselling. They felt that their multilingualism increased their attunement to other languages. They believed that they were able to get alongside other multilinguals more quickly, even if they did not share their languages, and that they were able to adapt rapidly to different accents and modes of speech. As one said:

> I can relate to their [the clients'] foreignness so they are more relaxed and trusting... I don't know whether this has something to do with language or whether my understanding of language has enabled me also to relate to very different philosophies and cultures, even those whose language I do not speak. (2010: 19)

They said it helped that they could understand when people were struggling to find the right words in their newly acquired English:

> I know how people may take verbs away or prepositions. I still have problems myself! (2010: 20).

With Jean-Marc Dewaele, I conducted another study of the beliefs, attitudes and practices of 101 monolingual and multilingual therapists with their multilingual patients (Costa & Dewaele, 2012). In the interview section of the study, one of the participating multilingual therapists attributed her ability to be more attuned to people's levels of understanding to learning and knowing different languages:

> I think that, if you have to learn various languages for whatever reason, you become much more attuned to what the other person is saying, to try to understand, because... you know what

it's like to be a foreigner or in a foreign situation, so you can make
that effort and you can be more flexible. You are more attuned
to whether people understand or don't understand. (Costa &
Dewaele, 2012: 29)

This therapist went on to describe vividly how she was able to pick up
cues that someone wasn't really understanding what was being said,
and how she would act on the cues:

I suppose it's sort of a dead-like hue in the eye that they haven't
really understood or they haven't caught the thought and
followed it in their own mind... I guess I check more... if they've
understood or if we've arrived at the same conclusion. (2012: 29)

The therapists in my 2010 study also felt that the language differential
could influence the power dynamics in the counselling room. This
could be unsettling, as described earlier, but it could also function as
an equaliser of power. Some counsellors reported that this frequently
occurred when their clients were more fluent in English than they
were:

I also think that when people realise English is not my first
language either, that changes the balance of power. (Costa, 2010:
19).

This shift in power differentials could be used positively and creatively.
For example, a Turkish-speaking therapist who trained in English and
offers therapy in English may feel judged because of her accent and
grammar. She may feel she loses her clinical authority when she works
with 'native' English speakers. On the other hand, she may feel able
to use her lack of familiarity with English colloquial expressions in a
playful and creative way (Costa & Dewaele, 2012:30), and so further
the therapeutic effect:

I was working with an [English] couple and she'd referred to her
mother as being a fishwife. I said, 'I don't understand really well,
but what is a fishwife?'... [Not being English] allows me to ask that
question. Probably I found out things that maybe a monolingual
wouldn't have been able to find out in that way. (2012: 30)

The counsellors in my 2010 study felt that clients' multilingualism meant they had access to a wider range of different emotions because they had a greater range of expression with their range of languages. For example, sometimes a client might find it difficult to get angry in English but the emotional connection would start to unlock in another language. One of the counsellors I interviewed said:

> People can feel a bit freer to speak about something that may be taboo in their language. For example, if expression of anger was not allowed when you were growing up, you may find that you can access and express this emotion in another language, which you have learned after your early, formative years. (2010: 19)

The counsellors also referred to linguistic agency. Some specifically stressed the importance for new arrivals to use the main host language of that country in counselling, as it gave them a greater sense of belonging and confidence:

> In some cases, it has increased their [the client's] confidence. For example, if they are new arrivals to this country, by trying to express their emotions in English gives them confidence to converse in English outside and has increased their cultural awareness of Britain. (2010: 20)

Some counsellors even felt that using English in counselling gave clients a chance to practise their English in a safe and non-judgemental environment, and thereby had a therapeutic benefit:

> … a client who is put down by her family for her English but the therapist says I can understand you enough… this has helped her a lot with her self-esteem, self-identity and confidence about speaking. (2010:19)

Interestingly, the counsellors highlighted the significance of linguistic empathy – their personal understanding of the effort that clients are making when they have to use English as their lingua franca in counselling.

They also felt comfortable with clients using different languages in the room, even if they were languages they did not understand. One counsellor commented:

> In some cases, when clients can't find any similar words in English, they may use phrases or words from their language that I may not be able to understand but it allows them to express the emotion. (2010: 21)

In keeping with Alison Phipps' (2019: 28) encouragement to enter into 'the unknowable, until one is over on the other side', several of the counsellors mentioned trying to learn a little of a client's language to use in the sessions. This could contribute to a positive therapeutic relationship and, again, could bring a momentary role reversal in the power dynamics:

> Most clients really appreciate that I am making an effort and also feel cared for. It… gives them confidence because they then take on a teaching role sometimes and correct my language. (Costa, 2010:19)

Bowker and Richards (2004) found that, while monolingual therapists might feel a sense of inferiority because of the linguistic ability of their multilingual clients, multilingual therapists do not share this experience. Echoing this, the therapists in our 2012 study said their clients' multilingualism did not make them feel anxious. They did not feel they had to apologise or feel guilty about their language limitations. However, they did highlight three major sets of challenges raised by their multilingualism: finding their professional identity in more than one language, boundary setting across languages, and over-identification/avoidance of multilingualism, all of which are echoed in other studies (Verdinelli & Biever, 2009; Costa, 2010; Costa & Dewaele, 2012). I will unpack each of these below.

Professional identity in more than one language

Some research studies (Verdinelli & Biever, 2009; Costa & Dewaele, 2012; Nguyen, 2014) have found that multilingual therapists often feel isolated and disconnected. They may be used to using two or more languages in their personal lives but many struggle to learn how to use more than one language (usually the one they trained in) in their professional lives (Verdinelli & Biever, 2009). As previously noted, multilingual therapists may be recruited for their language skills and therefore expected to be able to work in different languages by managers who have no understanding of the complexity of the task (Costa & Dewaele, 2012).

As we have already seen, many multilingual therapists feel they only have a professional identity in the language in which they were trained. They sometimes feel like a fraud when they work in other languages. There is often a pull into a more social rather than professional relationship when working in a shared minority language with a client. And, because they have received all their training and their own therapy in English, they may choose not to work in their primary language because it makes them feel deskilled.

Below is a case example I use in training sessions.

Case example

A counsellor has been allocated a Punjabi-speaking client. The counsellor speaks Punjabi but he did all his training in English. He feels he lacks the confidence to work with this client in Punjabi, although he is aware that his manager wants him to do so as it will save the cost of an interpreter. He asks his supervisor for advice about what he should do. His supervisor encourages him to say no if he does not feel confident to work in Punjabi.

When we discuss this case, an important point is often raised about the role that clinical supervisors play in keeping the organisational perspective in mind and supporting their clinical supervisees to be assertive when they feel that they are subject to unreasonable or unethical demands. While this is, without doubt, often appropriate, it is also important to think about the wider costs and consequences of the decision of this counsellor not to work in Punjabi. The simple solution is for the supervisor to support the supervisee not to work in Punjabi. But if clinical supervisors stay within what they regard as the limits of their intervention, they will simply maintain the status quo. This will probably occur when supervisors feel that they themselves do not feel confident to work constructively with multilingualism and psychological therapies. However, if they question the counsellor's decision and offer support and ways to develop their confidence to work in different languages, this will enhance multilingualism within the profession.

Thus, working within a multilingual therapeutic frame can help supervisors to see beyond the immediate organisational context. This broader landscape can include strategic and policy decisions about service development. I would argue that supervisors have a role to play in advocating for appropriate training for themselves and support for their multilingual supervisees to develop their professional multilingual identities.

Boundary setting across languages

Multilingual therapists have to think carefully about how they are going to frame the therapeutic work when working across languages. For example, language switching can occur in sessions, often without negotiation, on the part of either the client or the therapist. This can be for clarification or for inhibiting or amplifying expression and connection to feelings and a shared intimacy. The multilingual therapeutic frame enables the therapist to think about how, when and why the language switching occurs. Language switching is definitely worthy of recognition within the therapy, just as any other dynamic in the therapy room would be made conscious.

Therapeutic relationships, on the surface, have much in common with social relationships. The therapeutic frame helps us to keep the therapeutic relationship separate from the social frame. Through training and practice, we learn how to manage boundaries and how to phrase our interventions so that they provide a safe therapeutic frame for intimacy. In a social context, if a friend is distressed and starts to cry, we will probably want to offer comfort and reassurance. As a therapist, I have had to find new ways of expressing myself that differ from the ways in which I express myself socially. Like other people who have undertaken professional therapy training in the English language, the English expressions I have devised have helped form my professional identity. The expressions may not translate so well word for word into Punjabi, Swahili or Arabic, for example.

The frame allows other practices to become explicit, as the next case examples illustrate. Multilingual therapists may start a session with their multilingual clients with a casual and informal chat about everyday topics. Some languages differentiate formal and informal relationships by using different versions of the word for 'you'. So, for example, in French (and many other languages), there is an important distinction between 'tu' (informal, intimate) and 'vous' (formal, denoting respect for seniority). Punjabi-speaking counsellors tell me they often struggle to find the correct form of address for older female clients. Normally they might use 'Aunty' to signal respect, but, they say, somehow that does not seem appropriate in a counselling context.

What if a client starts to use a more intimate form of your name than you feel comfortable with? In Spanish, names are often adapted – Manolo for Manuel, Paco for Francisco, Trini for Trinidad etc. How would you respond to the client in a way that does not feel rejecting? These experiences can all affect the expectations clients have of the relationship.

At the beginning of this chapter we considered how not being able to speak the language of the country in which you are living can make someone feel vulnerable and infantilised. Clients who are not able to speak the host country's language are socially disempowered for a number of other reasons. They may be recently arrived refugees. They may have poor housing and employment prospects. Multilingual therapists can find themselves placed in the role of a care coordinator, following up on unresolved issues with social workers, housing departments and so forth. Here is an example from practice.

Case example

Sadia is an Arabic-speaking therapist working in a voluntary sector organisation in the UK. The charity provides free therapy and counselling for female survivors of domestic abuse. Sadia trained as a therapist in the UK, on a course delivered in English. She has been seeing an Arabic-speaking client for the past three weeks and their agreed plan involves her client attending an English language class or joining an exercise class. But Sadia's client doesn't speak enough English to find out about opening times and enrolment processes. Sadia is torn between finding out this information for her client or leaving her to find her own way. Sadia is pretty sure that, if she does not get her client this information, the client will not feel able to do it for herself.

Sadia grapples with the dilemma – is she empowering or disempowering her client if she finds this out for her? What impact does this 'extra role' have on the therapeutic relationship? These are all questions of ethical practice about client beneficence and client autonomy. Individual multilingual clinicians are often left on their own to make these difficult decisions if the additional linguistic pressure is not appreciated by managers and colleagues.

One way in which clinical supervisors and managers can help counsellors and therapists to address these issues is by thinking systemically about other local services available that could more appropriately offer this type of support. It is easy to forget the boundaries of the therapeutic frame when working multilingually. It can sometimes feel that you are the only person who speaks the client's language and are therefore the only person who can help. You may ask yourself, 'Why shouldn't I help, anyway? Aren't we all supposed to be acting with compassion in this profession?' The ethical dilemmas and the pull of compassion are examined again, and more widely, in Chapter 6.

Multilingual therapists often comment on how fast therapy can seem to be going when working with clients with a shared language. Both the therapist and the client may make assumptions about shared experiences. It is important that multilingual counsellors and therapists have sufficient, dedicated reflective space to consider whether or not they may be over-identifying with a client's vulnerability by becoming overly active (Perez Foster, 1998).

Here is one multilingual therapist's reflection, following supervision, about trying to balance acknowledgment of the client's appreciation for her effort and care with holding herself to account as a therapist, within the limitations of the role:

> But maybe there is a feeling of appreciation. There is so much appreciation that I'm giving my time to them and it's in Turkish, to get the service in Turkish… And they might also ask things from me, like, 'Can you do that for me? Can you write this letter for me? We are from the same place; can you do this favour for me?' And I… just explain what I can and what I cannot do. (Costa & Dewaele, 2012: 29)

One-to-one clinical supervision and supervision groups specifically focused on the task of multilingual working are important in helping to maintain the therapeutic frame.

Over-identification or avoidance

Antinucci (2004) identifies over-identification or over-joining with the client (Kokaliari, Catanzarite & Berzoff, 2013) as a common problem for multilingual therapists with multilingual clients. It may be a rare opportunity for the therapist to accompany someone who shares their home language and background on a nostalgic trip down memory lane.

Different languages can evoke visceral memories in all contexts, not just in therapeutic situations, as an example from my own experience illustrates. My father would often use a Greek endearment when he talked to me, calling me 'Beverleymou'. This is not a combination of sounds you hear very often. My father died 30 years ago and I had not heard that combination again until a couple of years ago, when a Greek friend addressed me in that way. Just hearing those familiar syllables, I felt a resonance throughout my body.

Therapists have described being taken back in time in a session, 'tasting' or 'smelling' food from childhood or remembering sounds and snatches of music, and then suddenly coming to, back in their present place, age and role. During that momentary lapse, the therapist has ceased to occupy their professional role and may have lost their professional footing. Conversely, multilingual therapists may unwittingly collude with clients who do not wish to speak in their first language because of their own sense of loss or conflict with their first language (Akhtar, 2006). Or they may feel a special attunement with a client who shares their linguistic history. Multilingual therapists tend to view their ability to share a language or their facility for languages as positive with respect to their capacity for attunement with a client. As one multilingual therapist commented in the research I conducted with Jean-Marc Dewaele (Costa & Dewaele, 2012):

> There is a kind of a familiarity that they (patients) experience with me, that probably they wouldn't with a (native) English speaker or through an interpreter… We know nobody else understands us, it's only us… probably more private, less threatening, less stressful, more relaxed. (2012: 28)

It is always important to hold any assumptions lightly. A facility for language can in fact have a negative impact on therapy, as the following story illustrates.

I had been working with a Spanish-speaking couple for three weeks. The couple had decisions they wanted to make about their future together and the final phase of their lives. Unusually for me, I had been letting sessions run over time. I seemed to lose track of time. I even found myself imagining the colour and the type of furniture in the couple's living room, and I was finding it hard to hold onto the reality of the people in front of me. I tried to reach for an explanation and an excuse for my behaviour. I was new to working with couples and I was tempted to blame my overrunning the sessions on my inexperience. But, at the periphery of my vision, I could just make out that the boundary transgressions were due to something else. With my supervisor, I tried to be as candid as possible. I considered my own needs to speak Spanish with this couple and how this was impacting on the course of therapy. By speaking with them in Spanish, I had allowed myself to become enmeshed with them in a nostalgic fantasy about their lives.

At the following session, I shared my concerns about letting the sessions run over time. It was a very fruitful discussion. From our conversation, we decided to continue in English as our lingua franca and to see how that affected the work. During the remaining sessions, we were able to hold the boundary together more effectively. The couple began to speak to each other directly, rather than via me. (I have to say that, until this experience, I would have expected this shift to have only occurred in the clients' first language.) The English language seemed to provide a containing function and to have a healthy distance and unmeshing effect for us all. It certainly helped me step away from over-identification and the nostalgic reverie and shared fantasy in which I had been engaging when speaking with the couple in Spanish. It also seemed to help the couple to face their own realities together.

Without the supervision from a supervisor who was experienced in thinking from within the multilingual therapeutic frame, we might have continued with the unexamined dynamic created by our language choice. Indeed, a less experienced supervisor who was not linguistically minded might have regarded the decision to work in Spanish as simply technical; they may not have understood the complex relational and dynamic issues involved.

Support and clinical supervision for multilingual therapists

Because of the specific challenges facing multilingual counsellors and therapists, services might want to think about setting up specific support structures for them. How do multilingual therapists learn the new language and identity of therapy if it does not happen during their training? It is often a difficult and lonely process. I suggest that there should be a place in initial training courses where this can occur, and not just for multilingual trainees; monolingual trainees too would benefit from training to work with multilingual clients in our increasingly multilinguistic world.

As a minimum, I would argue that agencies should set up specific supervision groups where multilingual therapists can share their dilemmas and learning. Such groups have been trialled successfully in some NHS IAPT services and voluntary agencies. The topics discussed include those explored above: maintaining boundaries; slipping into a social rather than a professional role; expectations from clients that their therapists will take on tasks outside their therapy role and making assumptions about shared experiences. Chapter 5 explores these supervision groups in more detail.

Conclusion

'The limits of my language are the limits of my world' (Wittgenstein, 1933). For therapists, like educationalists, one of our aims is to open up our clients to new possibilities and options while working within a contained frame. It seems that, for multilingual therapists and multilingual clients, their languages and language choices may indeed hold a key to enabling them to free themselves from what constrains them. Linguistic choices are dynamic and relational choices. They are a rich resource for therapists and clients.

In this chapter I have reviewed multilingual therapists' experiences and considered their specific skills, their sense of identity, the pushes and pulls inherent in working across languages and some possible appropriate support structures. Until very recently, clients' and therapists' multilingualism was hardly considered worthy of attention in the therapeutic encounter. But times are changing, or beginning to change, at least. At the end of her research paper on international counselling trainees' experiences, Lorena Georgiadou (2014) recommends that counselling courses pay more attention to languages and difference and that 'counsellor education programmes acknowledge the additional challenges that international trainees may encounter in practice in relation to linguistic competence and provide sufficient space and possibilities for relevant discussion with peers, tutors and supervisors' (2014: 9).

I began this chapter with the quote, 'I feel like a fraud.' Here is the context for that statement: it was said by a multilingual therapist who participated in the research interviews for the 2012 study mentioned above (Costa & Dewaele, 2012). She began the interview by talking about her technical capability in the language:

> Well, when I was thinking about coming to do this interview, I
> wondered whether I wasn't really a fraud, because although I do
> speak various languages, I've always been trained in only one, so
> when I tried to, even when people in Switzerland ask me about
> the kind of therapy I do, I find it incredibly difficult to explain,
> because I've never picked up a French textbook about CBT.

But less than an hour into the interview, her thinking had moved to a more relational evaluation of her multilingual identity as a therapist:

> … if you don't have the language and it's not tripping off your
> tongue and you're having to search for it, you're in the same
> position as the client. (2012: 29)

The opportunity to talk about multilingualism can significantly deepen people's appreciation about its role in therapy. In Chapters 4 and 5, I will consider some attempts to formalise these kinds of conversations about the multilingual therapeutic frame in suitable training and supervision to work with multilingualism, including interpreter-mediated therapy.

In Chapter 1, I claimed that monolingual and multilingual clients are different. There is no one fixed rule of practice that can be applied to this seemingly simple statement. It is sometimes preferable to work in a client's first language. But sometimes it is preferable to work in a client's other language(s). Often clients like to switch between their languages during a therapy session. And this may not be just for technical reasons; in the words of one multilingual therapist:

> There's a difference in what they're saying by switching, by
> saying, 'You know what I mean, I'm from this place.' So the act of
> switching is more important than the switch. (Costa & Dewaele,
> 2012: 30)

It is not always possible or practical to have a same-language therapist. It may not always be possible to work through an interpreter as there may not be one available, or a client may prefer not to have an interpreter. However, working with an interpreter can be a lifeline for some multilingual clients. We will consider interpreter-mediated therapy in the following chapter. As already stated, if we are committed to providing truly accessible services then we will need to find new ways of addressing the language gap between counsellors and clients. As one of the counsellors said in the interviews for my 2010 study:

> I have worked with many people from different cultures who use English as their way of communication here. It reflects the current state of society where differences are looking for a place to meet and to be understood. Counselling provides such an opportunity. (2010: 20)

References

Akhtar S (2006). Technical challenges faced by the immigrant psychoanalyst. *Psychoanalytic Quarterly* 75(1): 21–43.

Antinucci G (2004). Another language, another place: to hide or to be found? *International Journal of Psychoanalysis* 85: 1157–1173.

Apresjan J (1974). Regular polysemy. *Linguistics* 14(2): 5–32.

Biever J, Castaño MT, de las Fuentes C, González C, Servín-López S, Sprowls C, Tripp CG (2002). The role of language in training psychologists to work with Hispanic clients. *Professional Psychology: Research and Practice* 33(3): 330–336.

Bowker P, Richards B (2004). Speaking the same language? A qualitative study of therapists' experiences of working in English with proficient bilingual clients. *Psychodynamic Practice: Individuals, Groups and Organisations* 10(4): 459–478.

Caldwell-Harris CL (2014). Emotionality differences between a native and foreign language: implications for context-dependence and embodiment. *Frontiers in Psychology: language sciences;* 30 March. https://bu.academia.edu/CatherineCaldwellHarris/ (accessed 15 June 2020).

Costa B (2010). Mother tongue or non-native language? Learning from conversations with bilingual/multilingual therapists about working with clients who do not share their native language. *Journal of Ethnicity and Inequalities in Health and Social Care* 3(1): 15–24.

Costa B, Dewaele J-M (2012). Psychotherapy across languages: beliefs, attitudes and practices of monolingual and multilingual therapists with their multilingual patients. *Language and Psychoanalysis* 1: 19–41 (reprinted in *Counselling and Psychotherapy Research* 2014; 14(3): 235–244).

Georgiadou L (2014). 'My language thing… is like a big shadow always behind me': international counselling trainees' challenges in beginning clinical practice. *Counselling and Psychotherapy Research 14*(1): 10–18.

Imberti P (2007). Who resides behind the words? Exploring and understanding the language experience of the non-English-speaking immigrant. *Families in Society: the journal of contemporary social services 88*(1):67-73.

Kokaliari E, Catanzarite G, Berzoff J (2013). It is called a mother tongue for a reason: a qualitative study of therapists' perspectives on bilingual psychotherapy – treatment implications. *Smith College Studies in Social Work 83*(1): 97–118.

Nguyen B (2014). Identification: a qualitative study of the experiences of bilingual therapists with their monolinguals and bilingual clients. *Psychodynamic Practice 20*(4): 340–355.

Pavlenko A (2012). Affective processing in bilingual speakers: disembodied cognition? *International Journal of Psychology 47*(6): 405–428.

Perez Foster R (1998). *The Power of Language in the Clinical Process: assessing and treating the bilingual person.* Northvale, NJ: Aronson.

Phipps A (2019). *Decolonising Multilingualism: struggles to decreate.* Bristol: Multilingual Matters.

Shaw R (2003). *The embodied psychotherapist: the therapist's body story.* New York, NY: Brunner-Routledge.

Totton N (2015). *Embodied Relating: the ground of psychotherapy.* London: Karnac Books.

Verdinelli S., Biever JL (2009). Spanish-English bilingual psychotherapists: personal and professional language development and use. *Cultural Diversity and Ethnic Psychology 15*(3): 230–242.

Wittgenstein L (1933). *Tractatus Logico-Philosophicus.* New York, NY: Harcourt Brace.

3

Interpreter-mediated therapy

Working in this way doesn't come naturally (to therapists) and it almost feels as if they have lost some of their power. You end up having to say to the therapist: 'Can you please remember that you still have the power in the session?' (Interpreter)

Clients who need an interpreter can languish on waiting lists if counsellors and therapists don't want to work with interpreters. It isn't surprising that therapists can feel anxious about inviting a third person into the intimacy of the therapeutic dyad. It would be more surprising if they didn't. But there are therapists who welcome working with an interpreter and find that it can enhance the therapy.

In the previous chapters, we explored ways of working with multilingual clients directly, not mediated by an interpreter. Where counsellors and clients cannot be linguistically matched and there is no lingua franca, they will need to include an interpreter in their therapeutic relationship if they are going to be able to work together. Clients need to be able to have access to appropriately trained interpreters if they are truly going to experience equity of access to mental health services (Tribe & Lane, 2009). Asylum seekers interviewed by Bernardes and colleagues (2010) said they felt less inclined to use services if an interpreter was not available.

In this chapter, I will look at the challenges to effective interpreter-mediated therapy and how therapists can prepare so that they can work with clients who do not speak English as their first language. From the perspectives of client, interpreter and therapist, we will consider issues such as triadic relationships; anxiety and power; communicating about working methods; collaborative rather than competitive relationships, and clinical safety. Interpreters contribute a section in this chapter, describing what they need from therapists. I will then consider our duty of care towards interpreters and their support needs and conclude by recommending models of support for interpreters in the interpreter-mediated therapeutic relationship.

Preparing for interpreter-mediated therapy

Of course, not all clients want an interpreter, even if one is available. They may feel they will be judged if the interpreter is from their own community, or even in danger if the interpreter is from a hostile country, community or tribe. They may have concerns about having to trust another person, or overwhelmed by having to face two people in the room. They may feel their English is good enough and feel offended or humiliated by the offer of an interpreter. How is a therapist to handle this situation? Careful reflection and support in supervision can enable therapists to be reflective rather than reactive and active rather than passive. Preparatory work may be needed before the decision is made even to book an interpreter. For instance, the psychotherapist can check how the language need of the client was assessed, whether the client wants an interpreter, the availability of interpreters in the required language and so forth.

Case example

Marlene, a therapist, shares in a group supervision session that she is very concerned that she offended a client by offering him an interpreter. The client had responded to her offer crossly, saying that he did not need an interpreter. Marlene now feels embarrassed and says she doesn't want to bring this issue up again with the client, even though his English is poor and both she and he sometimes struggle to understand each other.

During the group supervision session, the group discusses how it might be possible in the next session for Marlene to ask the client to reflect with her on his response to the offer of an interpreter. Marlene agrees that it is possible that an exploratory conversation about the possible benefits and the client's feelings could be helpful.

At the next supervision session, Marlene reports that she felt more confident to broach the subject with the client in their next session.

She and the client had discussed Marlene's offer of an interpreter, both had been able to acknowledge their fears and assumptions and, at the end of the session, they agreed to try working with an interpreter. This conversation also enabled them to have other discussions about sensitive issues later in the therapy.

It is important to acknowledge that not all therapists will have access to an interpreter. There may not be an interpreter available who speaks a client's language or there may not be any funds to pay for an interpreter. Untrained interpreters and family members may be used as interpreters, which can compromise the integrity of the therapy. Although some researchers have expressed doubts about the use of friends and family members as interpreters, sometimes clients may want a family member or friend to interpret for them (Kuo & Fagan, 1999; Antonini, 2010). Antonini found that parents often prefer their children to interpret for them, even if other forms of language support are available:

> Because of cultural reasons, and for a host of other motives, immigrant parents will continue to ask their children to translate and interpret for them regardless of the law and of other resources available to them, such as professional interpreters and language mediators. (2010: 10)

In a review of users' experiences of access to services via interpreters, Alexander and colleagues found that this preference for friends and family may be because 'they trust them… they have an ongoing relationship with them and an emotional commitment and loyalty towards each other' (2004: 60). They also found that, when family members acted as interpreters, their role was to give both practical and emotional support, and this led to both positive and negative emotions.

However, for effective and ethical therapeutic work to take place, therapy needs to occur in a therapeutic frame (Gray, 2013) that contains difficulties and enables safety. The frame provides a space free from the external pressures of everyday life. This makes it unviable to work with a family member in the room (unless there is a contract to engage in family therapy that has been agreed by all those present – and the family member would not be taking the role of an interpreter).

So how can the therapist's wish to work only with a professional interpreter be reconciled with the client's wish to be interpreted for by a family member? Rejecting the offer of a family member to interpret requires delicate and sensitive communication. It is good to show appreciation and respect for the support offered, but it is advisable to stick to the professional boundary of not beginning therapy while a family member is present.

Case example

Maria was attending her first counselling session. But when Kamaljit, her counsellor, went to collect her from the waiting room, she was sitting with her sister, Ana. Ana explained to Kamaljit that she would be interpreting for Maria – she always did this and that is what Maria wanted. Kamaljit took them both into the therapy room, where an interpreter was waiting. Via the interpreter, Kamaljit thanked Ana for her support and explained that organisational policy meant that she would not be able to accept her kind offer. She asked Maria if she would be prepared to have one trial counselling session with the interpreter and they could then review together if she wanted to continue working in this way. Kamaljit also asked Ana if, later on, when the therapy had progressed, she could ask for her support, if relevant issues emerged in the sessions. This could include for example, asking Ana to accompany Maria to different, new activities. Maria and Ana agreed to give it a try.

It is easy for therapists to feel pulled into accepting a family member's kind offer to interpret. But, as therapists and counsellors, we need to think carefully about this kind of pull. It can feel counterintuitive and persecutory not to accept the offer of support. However, a psychotherapist with Mothertongue, Tamara Callea, reminds us to be wary of the urge to rescue:

> [Resisting the pull] involves a door closing on certain things. It is important not to give into the rescuer as, ultimately, it isn't creative. This is an area which is fraught with sharks. They aren't basking sharks either. (Personal communication)

Therapists and counsellors may worry about appearing culturally insensitive and ignoring families' preferences, values and systems. It is important to remember your reasons for making this decision. Do you actively want to involve a family member in the treatment? Is this part of your therapeutic plan? Or did you just slide into accepting the offer of help out of fear or because there was no alternative? It is important, even though it can be difficult, to stay active in the interpreter-mediated session, even when you do not understand what is being said.

Kamaljit demonstrates that she is making a conscious decision, not just reacting to a difficult situation. She uses the organisation's policy to move the discussion away from personal preferences. And, by treating Ana's offer with respect and giving some of the power back to her (by asking if she could contact her to ask for her help) and by not rejecting her completely, she is able to build enough trust for the session to go ahead appropriately.

In both of these case examples, Marlene and Kamaljit are thinking systemically. One of the keys to working successfully with an interpreter is to think about the system – what happens inside and outside the therapeutic conversation and the therapy room and what are the associated administrative tasks. Dynamic administration (Follett, 1940) refers to the essential administrative tasks that contribute to therapeutic containment and the potential for transformative experiences that therapy can provide. Thinking about the system starts before interpreter-mediated therapy even begins, as both these case examples illustrate.

I will now consider other preparatory work that is needed, again at a systemic level, before the interpreter is introduced. Most services and individual clinicians will need to access a professional interpreter through an agency. Agencies vary enormously in their charges, quality of service and treatment of the interpreters who work for them. It is well worth doing some research into the agencies in your area, to find the best ones. It is part of the systemic approach not only to do the research but also to act on your findings or feed your findings back to your service's commissioning managers, so that they can do so. It is important to be able to have good communication channels with the agency and for the agency to be responsive to your requests for specific genders, consistency of interpreters and appropriate language/dialect and so forth.

I will return to the systemic frame later in the chapter. But before we look at what happens in a session with the interpreter present, I will consider what may be going on in the minds of the three potential participants in the interpreter-mediated therapy session, even before it starts.

Three-sided fears

In the therapeutic triad of client, interpreter, counsellor, interpreters can be welcomed, grudgingly accepted or shunned by counsellors and clients (Boyles & Talbot, 2017; Tribe & Thompson, 2009). Power and safety are two major concerns for therapists working with interpreters. Clients may feel powerless and vulnerable. They are in a position where they need help and they cannot understand the language of their helper or make themselves understood in their own language. Therapists and counsellors can feel powerless to communicate directly and they are dependent on the interpreter for that communication to take place. Interpreters feel powerless, as they cannot make any independent intervention to alleviate the situation; they are reliant on the therapist to do that.

Powerlessness in interpreter-mediated helping situations can invoke a desire in professionals to compete with each other for control (Miller et al, 2005). A therapist or counsellor will be rightly concerned that they cannot guarantee that the therapy room is a safe space if they do not understand what is being said between the interpreter and client. They may also be concerned about establishing rapport with the client and staying in control of the session. Interpreters may be concerned that they will not understand any professional jargon used; that they may become emotionally overloaded by what they are expected to interpret, or that their own safety could be compromised. They may not trust the clinician if, for example, they are unfamiliar with the working methods of therapy. And clients may wonder if the interpreter will be able to translate their feelings accurately, or worry that they will breach confidentiality, or judge them, or even be from an opposing political faction. They may fear that their own voice will be lost.

With fears on the three sides of the triangle, it is not surprising that working with an interpreter in the room can feel daunting for practitioners and add an extra level of complexity to the therapeutic work. The therapist cannot directly understand what is being said in the room and yet they still hold clinical responsibility.

Ideally the practitioner and interpreter should feel that they are working on the same side, engaging in a team effort, rather than competing like rivals. Finding a way to work collaboratively in the service of clients is a priority for counsellors and interpreters. Bradford and Muñoz believe that in therapeutic work:

… the translator becomes an extension of the therapist […] the exercise of their respective roles entails momentary experiences of their sharing a single identity. (1993: 58)

This requires the clinician and the interpreter to prepare together and to work as a collaborative team. This means that the clinician needs to remain active throughout. But, because of the unconscious pushes and pulls, it is easy to believe you are staying active, when actually you have put yourself into a passive position, as this example demonstrates.

Case example

Gabriel is a counsellor who has started to work with an interpreter called Mabel. He isn't sure what went wrong in the session he has just delivered with Mabel. He felt he remained active, but he felt deskilled in the session. For example, at the briefing, he had told Mabel that, if the client spoke for a long time, Mabel should stop her and interpret back to him.

When he discusses it with his supervisor, Gabriel realises that, rather than staying active, he put himself into a passive position by giving the interpreter the responsibility for managing the client's communication flow. What looked like active behaviour actually disempowered him in the session. He had done that to himself!

Preparing systemically for interpreter-mediated therapy

I will now return to the practical, systemic preparations that can provide some solutions to these concerns and ensure that clinical safety and the support needs of interpreters and therapists are addressed.

1. Working as a collaborative team

Counsellors and therapists are more likely to achieve this if they meet alone with the interpreter first, before inviting the client to join them, so they can prepare for the therapy session, and de-brief together afterwards. Another essential element of the successful interpreter-mediated therapy session is respect and trust between the two professionals and for each other's working methods (Costa & Briggs, 2014; Hlavac, 2010). The pre-meeting is an opportunity for the therapist and interpreter to share their working methods with each other so that both parties understand the system within which they are working. Interpreters, like nature, abhor a vacuum. Unless you explain to the interpreter that you value silence and uninterrupted space (for example, for a client to cry), the interpreter may see it as their role to step in to keep the communication moving. Likewise, interpreters have observations that can help the therapist or counsellor. One interpreter told me in a pre-meeting:

> I wonder if therapists are aware that their 'therapist communication style' of tentative suggestions – eg. Would you like to think about...? etc – does not translate into some languages and leaves some patients feeling that the therapist is unsure of what they are doing.

As well as explaining their own working methods, the practitioner, while not relinquishing their clinical authority, listens to the interpreter's needs and the contribution they have to offer with their expertise. The practitioner and the interpreter's way of working together has been called a 'mini-*équipe*' (or mini-team) (Salaets & Balogh, 2015: 63). One tip that may help practitioners to feel more confident in the 'mini-*équipe*' is to remember that they hold the responsibility for the session.

2. Talking about the talking

Everyone needs to know the rules of communication at the very beginning of the session. You will need to decide whether you want the interpreter to interpret simultaneously (at the same time as you or the client are speaking) or consecutively (translating after each utterance). You will also need to decide if you want the interpreter to translate in the first or third person. There are pros and cons to any of these decisions and each therapist will need to choose what is best for their context.

Three-way communication through an interpreter differs systemically from dyadic communication. It might be helpful to set a communication ground rule before anyone says anything else: 'Everything that everyone says in the room will be interpreted.'

Likewise, you may want to discuss other aspects of communication within therapy. What will happen, for example, if the client wants to speak for a long time without interruption and you cannot understand what they are saying (the situation that Gabriel tried to manage in the previous case example)? Who takes the responsibility for managing this, and how do they do it? It is a problem for both the therapist and the interpreter. If the therapist doesn't manage it (by staying active), the interpreter will have to step in, or they will not be able to do their job effectively. Transparency is essential in all forms of counselling and psychotherapy but interpreter-mediated communication requires an unswerving commitment to keep everyone in the loop. Actively talking with all the participants in the triad about communication (or 'talking about the talking') is valuable in every therapeutic endeavour, but it is essential in three-way interpreter-mediated therapy.

3. Maintaining control of the session

Interpreters are trained and used to managing the communication flow in their work. This, however, gives an interpreter substantial control of the therapy session. As I have already said, the counsellor holds the clinical responsibility for the session. If they abdicate control of the communication flow to the interpreter, who then holds the responsibility?

Case example

Saira is an interpreter. She has had a pre-meeting with the counsellor, Ann. Ann has explained that she will set down all the ground rules about the communication. Saira waits patiently at the beginning of the session for Ann to explain that everything that everyone says will be interpreted, but Ann seems to have forgotten to mention this. Saira thinks this is too important to neglect and so she intervenes and explains the ground rule in both the languages of the counsellor and the client. Ann is cross with herself for forgetting to set the ground rule, and she is cross with Saira for interrupting.

Of course, as a therapist or counsellor, if we want the interpreter to trust us to hold the authority, we have to do what we have said we will do. This is an example of how quickly the counsellor can become passive, how control can slip away and how all kinds of anxieties get elicited and acted out on when mistakes are made, even when everyone's intentions are benign.

4. Thinking outside the box (room)

Receptionists will often seat interpreters and clients together in the waiting room. What are the potential unwanted consequences of that? Sitting next to the client, it is hard for interpreters to manage unboundaried conversations, where they may hear about safeguarding issues or they may need to refuse vulnerable clients' requests for their phone numbers. Similarly, if the interpreter and client leave together, it is understandable that the client may want to continue to talk to someone who speaks their language and appears to understand how the UK systems work. Systemic preparation by therapists and counsellors includes thinking about how interpreters arrive and leave appointments so they are not left on their own to manage unfacilitated conversations with clients.

5. Timing

It is helpful to think about possible extra time needed before the session begins. You may want to be able to offer extra or longer sessions, and you should check this with the interpreter first, bearing in mind that the interpreter will need a break after 45 minutes.

6. Seating and eye contact

Many counsellors find that a triangular seating arrangement favours an egalitarian approach to communication. Even when the interpreter is speaking to them, counsellors usually want to look at the client, in order to build and maintain rapport with them. It can be helpful to have explained this to the interpreter in the pre-meeting.

7. Reflecting on the triangular relationship

The interpreter-mediated therapy triad is not exempt from the pulls and pushes inherent in triangular relationships. Helping relationships layer their own power dynamics onto triangles. Our own histories of being in triangular relationships can trigger unhelpful behaviour. Self-reflexivity on the part of the therapist and the interpreter can help to bring these complexities into the light. They are then available, as part of the therapeutic material, to be thought about and worked with productively. Steve Karpman's (1968) Drama Triangle is relevant here. The three corners of the triangle are occupied respectively by the Persecutor, Victim and Rescuer. It is almost inevitable that the therapist and the interpreter will both gravitate towards the Rescuer role. The role of Victim may be experienced by anyone in the triangle. Although no member of the triangle may gravitate towards the Persecutor role, it will pull towards it anyone who is unaware of and/ or who discounts their own authority and power. A useful exercise (described in Chapter 4) for therapists and interpreters is to think of the triangular relationships they have been in over the course of their lives. It can then be helpful to focus on the patterns of inclusion and exclusion and the functional and dysfunctional coping strategies they have developed to help them manage anxieties that can be elicited in any triangular relationships. Without this self-examination, the dysfunctional personal coping strategies can be brought into the therapy room and enacted within the dynamics of the therapeutic triad (Costa, 2017a).

8. Be mindful of the interpreter's support needs

As well as making the therapist's own needs and the client's needs known to the interpreter, it helps if the therapist can stay mindful of the interpreter's needs. Interpreters work in unpredictable and emotionally charged contexts, with very little, if any, support. They really appreciate being briefed about what they are going into and debriefed at the end, so they can take stock. Without five to 10 minutes' space at the beginning and end of a session, they can be left 'emotionally naked' as they enter or leave a therapy session. It seems only fair to give the interpreter information, if it is available, so that they can prepare themselves for a distressing situation. Even in very busy contexts, briefing and debriefing is essential so that they have space to think and learn and so avoid burnout. Ideally, where possible, supervision groups should be set up for interpreters (Costa, 2017a, b, c).

I have included here a short code of practice and tips for interpreters and therapists. In the next section, we will look a little more closely at why interpreters need support and the form that support can take.

Good practice guide for clinicians working with interpreters[1]

ISSUES TO OBSERVE:

- Allow time for a pre-meeting with the interpreter to establish ways of working together.

- In the pre-meeting, explain to the interpreter your working methods and the outcomes you expect.

- Let the interpreter know if you will be using any specific or unusual terminology.

---

1. This is an abridged version of the code developed and used by Mothertongue

- Arrange the seating so that everyone can see each other.
- Clarify that you, the clinician, have ultimate responsibility for the session. The interpreter needs to feel able to trust you to hold that responsibility.
- In the session, speak directly to the client.
- Introduce yourself and the interpreter. Think how you will manage beginnings and endings of sessions –the interpreter and client should not be left alone together.
- Set the ground rules, including confidentiality and that everything spoken by everyone in the room will be translated out loud.
- Be transparent in how you work.
- Reassure the client their message and their voice are important and that you will do your best to listen very carefully to them.
- Explain that you will be regularly summarising and checking your understanding with the client.
- Reassure the client about interpreting accuracy/confidentiality.
- Speak in small meaningful chunks. Allow space for the interpreter to translate accurately.
- Be aware of cultural differences and check if and how your client experiences those differences.
- If the client can speak some English, discuss together, between the three of you, how the interpreter can be most useful in the session.
- Talk about the talking.
- Thank anyone from the family who wants to interpret so that they feel validated but explain that you are required to have a professional interpreter for your work. You may want to suggest that you might appreciate their support with other aspects of care if they are willing. It is important that the family member does not feel rejected or humiliated, for the wellbeing of everyone involved.
- Allow enough time to debrief the interpreter at the end.
- Prepare in advance to ensure that you allow enough time for the whole session. Be prepared for interpreter-mediated therapy to take longer and, if necessary, to need additional sessions.
- Work collaboratively with the interpreter.

ISSUES TO AVOID:

- Don't use jargon.
- Don't refer to the client in the third person.
- Don't hand responsibility for the session to the interpreter (or allow the interpreter to take over the session).
- Don't leave the interpreter and the client alone together.
- Don't have a private conversation with the interpreter in the client's presence.
- Don't expect the interpreter to be your general assistant or to look after the client.

The support needs of interpreters

Interpreters' susceptibility to vicarious trauma and burnout

Interpreters are the voice of their clients and they often leave sessions with terrible memories and thoughts that are hard to put down. Clients who need an interpreter can have harrowing stories to tell. They may have arrived in the UK seeking asylum, having endured terrible journeys as well as persecution in their home country. Interpreters run the same, perhaps even greater, risks as other frontline workers of developing vicarious trauma and burnout.

> Those of us who've served as interpreters in everyday life know it's a bittersweet privilege. You find truths in the in-between spaces of language, but never the right words to express them. You hear the sound of someone being heard in your voice, and the sound of someone being unseen in the silence. You speak of simple things, hard things and joyous things, all diluted by the separation from their source. It will never seem fair that a person's words are not enough. (Sylvester, 2019).

Clients need to trust their interpreter, who will be voicing their sensitive stories. For this reason, interpreters aim to form an empathic relationship with their clients. This leaves them vulnerable to vicarious trauma, which results from their empathic engagement with a client's trauma material (Valero Garces, 2015; Pearlman & Saakvitne, 1995). Interpreters may also be susceptible to moral injury, a concept that has emerged from research with combat veterans. Moral injury results from being involved in or witnessing distressing events that transgress your moral code, yet you are unable to offer direct relief to those who are injured (Litz et al, 2009).

Interpreters are often in the position of bystander, witnesses to horror and unable (because of the professional and ethical limitations of their role) to do anything about it. This can be exacerbated when clients' stories of trauma and terror resonate with interpreters' own experiences. Interpreters can end up feeling as helpless as the teller of the story.

But interpreters have little if any help with self-care and there are few outlets for them to process the emotional impact of their work (Boyles & Talbot, 2017). They are seldom provided with support to prevent burnout (Doherty, MacIntyre & Wyne, 2010; Costa & Briggs 2014; Costa, 2017c). Therapists need to think about how we can help interpreters to manage the emotional challenges of the work; managers should ensure there is funding to provide this help included in the overall cost of interpreting services. It is an additional cost in the short term, but in the long term there is cost saving because there will be fewer absences and resulting cancelled appointments.

Support can be offered to interpreters one-to-one (Costa, Lázaro-Gutiérrez & Rausch, 2020) or through a supervision group (Costa, 2017b). One-to-one supervision can be particularly suitable for interpreters working in specialised contexts. Group supervision is more cost effective but it may also be more helpful: interpreters often value the opportunity to share experiences and find solutions together, as (like counsellors) they frequently work on their own.

Supervision of interpreters serves three functions: reparative, reflexive and responsive. The reparative function combines features of professional and pastoral mentoring; the reflexive function is akin to clinical supervision, and the responsive function supports interpreters' exploration of systemic and organisational changes. This model is described in more detail in Chapter 5. This is how one interpreter, who I interviewed for a film about supervision, described the support they derived from their supervision group:

> You can get home and it (the interpreting assignment) can impact on the relationship you have with friends and family. Because, if you don't offload here, it's going to come out. And sometimes in the wrong situations.

Another interpreter from the same group said that, while a debrief straight after a session was useful, it might not be enough:

> Most clinicians will offer some support at the end of the session. You can't always remember, you can't always think, because during the session you're there 100%, trying to be professional. You don't let your emotions get in the way; you keep them buckled down.

The interpreter's perspective

An interpreter may have had experiences of sitting through therapy sessions that were well run but where the practitioner used methods with which the interpreter was not familiar. Or they may have witnessed genuinely poor practice and have serious concern for the client. It may have been hard for the interpreter to tell one situation from the other if the practitioner has not explained their methodology to them.

The following excerpt is from a story by Guida Shields, in an anthology of interpreters' stories called *In Other Words*, collected by Mothertongue (Hayman & Costa, 2015). The anthology gives some insight into interpreters' experiences and dilemmas about intervening when they feel that clients are being disadvantaged by a service. The excerpt is from an anonymous and amalgamated story about interpreting for a children's service at a group meeting of professionals.

Although the context is not psychological therapy, the interpreter's experience is relevant to therapeutic work. In the story, the interpreter sits next to the mother for whom she is interpreting. The meeting has been called to decide whether the woman's three-year-old son is to be returned to her or remain in care.

> As I sat next to her, I could see the clenching and unclenching of her hands, nails bitten to the quick. If only I could soften the delivery of what was being said. Everything that is being said must be interpreted. How many times had I heard that, how many times had I repeated it? Knowing it is the right way does not make it any easier.
>
> Words by themselves are easy to interpret, but it is what's hidden behind them that is so very hard to convey. Like a football spectator, I am the only one who can see both sides of the field. I

watch both teams playing their game and only I am in a position to understand both sides. Each side relies on me, but all I am translating are the words. There is so much more, unseen by them, that I have to bottle up.

Although what was being said came from other mouths, it was from mine that she heard it. It made me feel like the executioner pulling the trigger. The words I was uttering were having the same deadly effect. (2015: 35)

The excerpt paints a graphic picture of this interpreter's experience. What follows is an amalgamation of the experiences, perspectives and suggestions of a number of interpreters who worked for Mothertongue – Guida Shields, Kamaljit Dosanjh, San Maya Gurung, Joanna Mungai, Soumaya Elhabarri and Dalia Arab – in their own voices. These experiences were collected during the research phase of the co-creation of *Between*, the first production of a performance company of interpreters and practitioners called Around the Well, which is based within the Pásalo Project and the Department of Film, Theatre & Television at the University of Reading.

Sometimes you can think things are going very well. I once interpreted in a session that felt like two sides of a coin. Half the session went really well. But then, in the second half of the session, the clinician invited the client's sister in, and they started to have a private conversation. The clinician didn't want this interpreted for the client, but it was very awkward. The client kept looking at me and I didn't know what to do. I think, if they wanted to have a private conversation, they should have done that when the patient and I weren't in the room. The clinician didn't tell me what he needed me to do, whether I should interpret, whether I should leave the room. He just ignored me. When this has happened again, I have had to ask the clinician what they wanted me to do and to suggest that they explain what is happening to the client. Sometimes they just expect me to have a conversation with the client while they discuss some issues with the family members.

We end up having to train the clinicians as we are going along. I once worked with a clinician who kept saying to me 'Can you ask her…? Can you tell her …?', and so in the debrief I said 'Would you mind if I offer some feedback? In the session it is so much nicer for the client if they think you are engaging directly with them. Don't worry about me.'

And sometimes the whole session can be disastrous. I had an awful experience once. I was doing a telephone session with a clinician and the client. There was no introduction. Nothing. Just silence. I wondered if the phone connection was OK. And, after a long while, I heard some laughing and I said: 'Hello. My name is X and I am the interpreter. You may go ahead when you are ready.' The clinician then replied over the phone, 'Interpreter. I don't like this tone.' I didn't know what to do. With the client there, I couldn't say anything to him. I carried on interpreting for the rest of the session, but I was shaking. There was nothing I could do.

If we have the briefing session, we can explain to the clinician about everything that should happen: to explain to the patient about confidentiality; that everything that is said will be interpreted; remind them of speaking in small chunks and normally. If that is said, if the clinician is good, they will carry it through. I did that recently and, so far, they have seated me and the client separately; they don't leave us alone together at the end of the session.

When we don't have a briefing session with the clinician, the session itself often doesn't go very well and then the client is left unsatisfied. And when we don't have a briefing session, I feel like I have lost some power. For instance, I was interpreting for a male client who kept turning to me and looking at me and the clinician kept repeating to the client, 'Can you look at me? Can you look at me?', several times. And so the client had to stop and several times he lost what he was going to say. Many times. Not just once. In the end I came out of the session and I felt very dissatisfied; I thought neither the clinician nor the patient understood each other, and both were unhappy.

But sometimes it can work very well. I remember at the end of the first session with a clinician she said: 'Oh my God. I am worn out. I didn't realise there were so many things to think about when working with an interpreter.' And, until then, I hadn't thought about it from the therapist's point of view, actually. Working in this way doesn't come naturally [to therapists] and it almost feels as if they have lost some of their power. You end up having to say to the therapist: 'Can you please remember that you still have the power in the session?'

Therapists can often give their authority away. They rely on us for too much or they forget to take care of some of the things. Sometimes clinicians don't realise that they need to manage the endings better, beyond what goes on in the room. I can do it but then they lose some of their authority and their management of the boundaries. I once had a client who wanted to talk to me and would linger outside the venue. I had to find ways of staying inside so that I didn't have a conversation with her outside the session.

We have to deal with clinicians' experiences of having had unqualified and inexperienced interpreters who are not professional. We have lost respect because of other interpreters who bring us into disrepute. Agencies use poor interpreters because the pay is so bad, good interpreters won't work for them.

You can go to an appointment and at the beginning the clinician does not seem very pleased to see you, and then at the end of the session there is a sigh of relief and they say, 'Oh, that is how it is supposed to work.' One therapist told me that she had had to stop one session and ask the interpreter to leave because they kept interfering; they were trying to run the session. That is of course wrong, but we also have a huge responsibility as an interpreter. Sometimes the clinician is lost. They don't know where to sit, how we are going to start… Not everyone can interpret. This is a profession. Maybe we should not be paid as much as doctors because they have the clinical responsibility. But the pay reflects the respect we have. The lower you are paid, the less respect you have. It is a profession and we need to remember that. We should be rewarded, not the same as doctors, because the qualification is different, but we should be treated as a professional. The pay certainly gives a message to everyone that there is an equivalence of respect for what we are doing. They need to think of us as colleagues.

Conclusion

Finding a way to work collaboratively in the service of clients is a priority for counsellors and interpreters and ultimately a benefit for all. It will be difficult for interpreters to discern between good and bad practice unless we, the therapists, share our working methods with interpreters. If we think of interpreter-mediated therapy as a system and we broaden our thinking beyond the dyadic relationship within a therapy room, we will be better prepared to consider wider issues. These issues include our role and relationship with interpreting agencies and our commitment to preparation. We need to think about how a client and an interpreter find their ways to and from the consulting room, and how we treat an interpreter as a valued and respected fellow professional while holding the control and the clinical authority at all times.

And throughout all of this, we are subject to the pushes and pulls of the Drama Triangle. While counsellors and therapists have clinical supervision to help them think about all of these issues, interpreters almost never have access to this type of support. We might want to think about how we can exercise our duty of care towards interpreters, especially as they are often exposed to the risk of vicarious trauma and burnout.

Finally, in this chapter, we heard the interpreters' own voices. I hope this inspires therapists to want to hear what the interpreters they work with think. Collaboratively, therapists and interpreters can think about what is needed for interpreter-mediated therapy to be effective and for it to play its part in reducing inequality of access to counselling and therapy services.

In the next chapter I will look at training to equip therapists to work with multilingual clients, with and without an interpreter.

References

Alexander C, Edwards R, Temple B (2004). *Access to Services With Interpreters: user views*. York: Joseph Rowntree Foundation.

Antonini R (2010). The study of child language brokering: past, current and emerging research. *mediAzioni 10*: http://mediazioni.sitlec.unibo.it/index.php/no-10-special-issue-2010.html (accessed 15 June 2020).

66   *Other Tongues*

Bernardes D, Wright J, Edwards C, Tomkins H, Dlfoz D & Livingstone AG (2010). Asylum seekers' perspectives on their mental health and views on health and social services: contributions for service provision using a mixed-methods approach. *International Journal of Migration, Health and Social Care* 6(4): 3–19.

Boyles J, Talbot N (2017). *Working with Interpreters in Psychological Therapy.* London: Routledge.

Bradford D, Muñoz A (1993). Translation in bilingual psychotherapy. *Professional Psychology Research and Practice* 24(1): 52-61. DOI: 10.1037/0735-7028.24.1.52

Costa B (2017a). Team effort – training therapists to work with interpreters as a collaborative team. *International Journal for the Advancement of Counselling* 39(1): 56-69. doi:10.1007/s10447-016-9282-7

Costa B (2017b). The strength and the stress of triangles: support and supervision for interpreters and therapists. In: Boyles J (ed). *Psychological Therapy with Torture Survivors in Exile; a human rights approach.* Monmouth: PCCS Books (pp 331-350).

Costa B (2017c) The challenges of interpreting in mental health settings. [Blog.] Terminology Coordination; 4 July. http://termcoord.eu/2017/07/the-challenges-of-interpreting-in-mental-health-settings/ (accessed 28 July 2019).

Costa B, Briggs S (2014). Service-users' experiences of interpreters in psychological therapy: a pilot study. *International Journal of Migration, Health and Social Care* 10(4): 231–44. doi: 10.1108/IJMHSC-12-2013-0044.

Costa B, Lázaro-Gutiérrez R, Rausch T (2020). Self-care as an ethical responsibility: a pilot study on support provision for interpreters in human crises. *Translation and Interpreting Studies* 15(1): 36–56. doi: https://doi.org/10.10785/tis.20004.cos

Doherty SM, MacIntyre AM, Wyne T (2010). How does it feel for you? The emotional impact and specific challenges of mental health interpreting. *Mental Health Review Journal* 15(3): 31-44.

Follett MP (1940). *Dynamic Administration: the collected papers of Mary Parker Follett* (Fox EM, Urwick L, eds). London: Pitman Publishing.

Gray A (2013). *An introduction to the therapeutic frame.* Hove: Routledge.

Hayman S, Costa B (eds) (2015). *In Other Words.* Reading: Mothertongue.

Hlavac J (2010). Ethical implications in situations where the language of interpretation shifts: the AUSIT Code of Ethics re-visited. *Translation & Interpreting* 2(2): 29–43.

Karpman S (1968). Fairy tales and script drama analysis. *Transactional Analysis Bulletin* 7(26): 39-43.

Kuo D, Fagan,MJ (1999). Satisfaction with methods of Spanish interpretation in an ambulatory care clinic. *Journal of General Internal Medicine* 14(9): 547–550.

Litz BT, Stein N, Delaney E, Lebowitz L, Nash WP, Silva C, Maguen S (2009). Moral injury and moral repair in war veterans: a preliminary model and intervention strategy. *Clinical Psychology Review* 29(8): 695–706. doi: 10.1016/j.cpr.2009.07.003

Miller KE, Martell ZL, Pazdirek L, Caruth M, Lopez, D (2005). The role of interpreters in psychotherapy with refugees: an explanatory study. *The American Journal of Orthopsychiatry* 75(1): 27–39. doi:10.1037/0002-9432.75.1.27

Pearlman L.A, Saakvitne KW (1995). Treating therapists with vicarious traumatization and secondary traumatic stress disorders. In: Figley C (ed). *Compassion Fatigue: coping with secondary traumatic stress disorder in those who treat the traumatized.* New York, NY: Brunner/Mazel (pp150-177).

Salaets H, Balogh K (2015). Co-Minor-IN/QUEST research findings. In: Balogh K, Salaets H (eds). *Children and Justice: overcoming language barriers. Cooperation in interpreter-mediated questioning of minors.* Cambridge-Antwerp-Portland: Intersentia (pp175–326).

Shields G (2015). Round table. In: Hayman S, Costa B (eds). *In Other Words.* Reading: Mothertongue (pp34–39).

Sylvester N (2019). The beauty of being bilingual. *The New York Times*; 20 September. www.nytimes.com/2019/09/20/opinion/bilingual-children.html (accessed 21 September 2019).

Tribe R, Lane P (2009). Working with interpreters across language and culture in mental health. *Journal of Mental Health 18*(3): 233–241. DOI: 10.1080/09638230701879102

Tribe R, Thompson K (2009). Exploring the three-way relationship in therapeutic work with interpreters. *International Journal of Migration, Health and Social Care 5* (2): 13–21.

Valero Garcés, C (2015). The impact of emotional and psychological factors on public service interpreters: preliminary studies. *Translation and Interpreting 7*(3): 90–102.

4

Training to work with multilingualism in psychological therapies

Therapy should not always be about white, middle class people;
we need to ensure access to therapy for all. (Training participant)

I have already talked about the potential to view multilingualism in
therapy as a purely technical skill. If multilingualism features at all in
training programmes, it is often as a technical question: for example,
'How do you talk about depression if there isn't a word for depression
in a client's language?' or 'Where is the best place for the interpreter
to sit?' These are relatively simple problems to resolve. As I have
pointed out, the impact of multilingualism on people's psychological
development and experiences does not feature in the curriculum
as one of the core competencies and capabilities in counsellor and
therapist training courses.

In Chapter 1, I suggested some reasons why multilingualism elicits
anxieties for therapists at the relational level. Feelings of exclusion are
inevitable when you do not understand what someone is saying. For
monolinguals, there can be a sense of shame or inferiority when clients
speak several languages with great fluency. Equally, multilinguals
can easily assume that, because they speak more than one language,
they understand any multilingual client's experience. A multilingual
therapist once told me that she didn't feel she needed to attend a
training session on linguistically sensitive therapy as she was already
working regularly in her three languages – English, French and

Spanish. I asked her how she thought therapeutically about the needs of her Punjabi-speaking clients, with whom she worked in English as a lingua franca. Did she think, for example, that their sense of self might be different when they were speaking their different languages and how did she attend to that in the sessions? She thought for a moment and then replied that she thought she had better attend the training session after all.

I am not alone in recommending training for therapists and counsellors in how to work collaboratively with interpreters (Boyles & Talbot, 2017; Costa, 2011, 2017a; Costa & Briggs, 2014; Salaets & Balogh, 2015; Tribe & Thompson, 2009). Therapy trainings are also ideally placed to address the deeper relational and process aspects of working across languages. Relational processes underpin all models of therapy. That is why the training described in this chapter is not modality specific. Linguistic issues also underpin all models of counselling and psychotherapy, and this too is reflected in the experience of participants in the training programmes described in this chapter. For example, Bager-Charleson and colleagues (2017) report one training participant's reflection, after the training, that she needed to expand her CBT approach to include other therapeutic modalities and adapt her usual method of having a set agenda:

> [But] I kept thinking, I don't have an answer, I just know it's going to be painful whatever you do, it's going to be very tough… it's difficult being in-between. (p69)

This chapter is aimed at managers of counselling and psychotherapy services and training institutes who can institute the necessary changes in their training programmes and supervision provision. It is also aimed at individual therapists, so that they know what to look for when they are searching for training courses and supervision that can equip them to work with multilingualism in the therapy room.

Culturally competent or culturally sensitive capabilities are now enshrined in most counselling and psychotherapy training curricula and frameworks – for example, and most recently, the draft framework setting out shared standards for education and practice produced by the British Association for Counselling and Psychotherapy (BACP), the British Psychoanalytic Council (BPC) and the United Kingdom Council for Psychotherapy (UKCP) as part of the SCoPEd collaboration (BACP, BPC, UKCP, 2018). This framework specifies the abilities to incorporate the consideration of client or patient cultural values into ethical decision-making and to demonstrate an awareness of how one's own culture will impact on the therapeutic relationship. However, nowhere is multilingualism mentioned specifically. It tends to be subsumed under the category of culture.

Of course, culture and multilingualism are inextricably linked. The problem for multilingualism is that culture tends to take up all the oxygen when they are considered together. Culture is a huge and important topic. But in order to preserve some airtime for multilingualism in training programmes and supervision, it can be useful to bracket it off artificially, examine it as a distinct phenomenon, before integrating it back among the whole raft of issues pertaining to culture and their implications for therapeutic work. The training programmes and the supervision and training of supervisors described in this chapter inevitably include some aspects relating to cultural awareness, but there is a clear line drawn around multilingualism and its specific impact and the relevant interventions in therapy.

In the preface, I mentioned that I had set up Mothertongue, a linguistically and culturally sensitive counselling service, and that I had run it, with an excellent team, for several years. We had plentiful opportunities to see first-hand that there were gaps in the training to prepare therapists to work effectively with the client groups we were seeing. This led us to set up our own training and supervision programmes, which were further developed and improved with the input from the findings from our subsequent research. The training and supervision programmes formed the second phase of the three-phase project mentioned in Chapter 1. In the third phase, we evaluated the training, and some of those findings are mentioned in this chapter. The specific phases are reported on more fully in a joint paper I wrote with Jean-Marc Dewaele (Costa & Dewaele, 2019).

Two training programmes will be described in this chapter: multilingualism and therapy/counselling, and training to work with interpreters in therapy and counselling. The duration of the training programmes can range between 1.5 hours and two days – the programmes are designed to be flexible so they can be offered in a variety of timeframes. Groups sizes range between five and 60, and the content is aimed at both trainees and experienced clinicians, training together.

Multilingualism and therapy/counselling

This training programme is based on the findings from research demonstrating that multilingualism can be a therapeutic asset. To summarise:

- a multilingual client is different from a monolingual client
- most multilinguals feel like a different person in their different languages (Dewaele, 2016; Panicacci & Dewaele, 2017)
- people are able to express different emotions in different languages (Dewaele, 2013)
- multilinguals can use their different languages to process trauma – moving towards emotional intensity in one language, or protecting themselves from becoming overwhelmed by their emotions in another (Tehrani & Vaughan, 2009)
- early memories can only be accessed and recalled in depth in the language in which they were experienced (Schrauf, 2000)
- language-switching in therapy can allow clients to express themselves more completely (Bager-Charleson et al, 2017).

The aim of the training is to build monolingual and multilingual therapists' skills and confidence to work within the multilingual therapeutic frame (with and without an interpreter). Participants are encouraged to explore how multilingualism can be used as a therapeutic asset and how to put this into practice in therapeutic work with multilingual clients. The focus of the training is on the process and relational implications of working therapeutically across languages. The training is structured around the principles of linguistic empathy, agency and privilege (see Chapter 1).

The training programme uses case examples to illustrate the themes, prompt discussion and encourage creative ideas about possible therapeutic responses to the vignettes. It includes questions that are frequently asked by therapists working with multilingual clients. It also uses films, creative writing exercises, hot-seating and other methods drawn from psychodrama, forum theatre and drama toolkits.

The impact of the training and supervision projects was evaluated formally with a group of 88 participants, who had received the training, between 2014 and 2016 (Bager-Charleson et al, 2017). The aim of the evaluation was to establish, through a questionnaire and interviews, the effect and impact of the training on the work of psychotherapists with multilingual patients. The quotations from participants in this chapter are taken from the open box responses in the research questionnaire and interviews, unless indicated otherwise. The exercises are intended to provide a snapshot of the interactive nature of the training.

Linguistic empathy, agency and privilege

Linguistic agency has two components: the speaker's reasonable command of the productive language and the listener's willingness to try to decode what they are hearing. In No Violet Bulawayo's novel *We Need New Names* (2013), which is set in Zimbabwe and the US, she comments on the two-way process of linguistic agency. First, she describes the speaker's activity:

> … first you have to think what you want to say. Then you have to carefully arrange those words in your head. Then you have to say the words quietly to yourself, to make sure you got them okay. And finally, the last step, which is to say the words out loud and have them sound just right.

But, she explains, despite your best efforts, you can still end up sounding like 'you are speaking like falling'. Next, she describes the consequences for the speaker's linguistic agency if the monolingual listener does not fulfil their responsibility to listen adequately:

> The problem with those who speak only English is this: they don't know how to listen; they are busy looking at your falling instead of paying attention to what you are saying. (2013: 194)

This 'looking at your falling' is what the receptionist does in the following exercise.

Exercise 1: Looking at your falling

Aim: this exercise is intended to give participants a sense of the disempowerment, frustration and infantilisation experienced when someone is trying to communicate in a language they barely understand or speak. The exercise highlights a number of issues about agency, power and bias.

The group, collectively, is given the role of carer of a sick 18-month-old child. The carer has recently arrived in a foreign country. They do not speak the language of this country except for the three words they have been taught: babu (child), cafor (hot), doctora (doctor). They are asked to try to convince a sceptical GP receptionist that they need an urgent appointment for their sick child, using only these three words. The trainer plays the unhelpful receptionist.

Participants respond to the exercise in a number of ways. They generally use a wide repertoire of gestures and body language (some have even resorted to crying and pulling at the receptionist), but the 'receptionist' is not kindly disposed to 'foreigners' and refuses to even try to understand. Participants report that they feel frustrated, infantilised, angry and powerless. They recognise the limitations of body language and how important it is that the listener is willing to make an effort to understand.

At the end of the exercise, participants are asked to give examples of how they will apply what they have learned in their practice. Comments usually reflect a growing realisation of how hard it is for people to communicate in English if it is not their first language. Participants describe the experience that some of their multilingual clients may have had in their everyday lives with listeners who, despite or because of their linguistically privileged position, are less than cooperative. It can be painful, delegitimising and demoralising to feel unable to communicate the complexity of our thoughts and emotions in a newly acquired language (Dewaele, 2016). Participants say this exercise is very helpful in developing their linguistic empathy.

Participants come up with various suggestions for interventions to address linguistic privilege in therapy sessions. For instance, one participant suggested he might ask his client: 'What is it like for you to talk to me about these very personal issues in English?' Other participants have said the training made them more mindful of the importance of linguistic empathy and the need to acknowledge the differential in effort when the language used in the sessions is their first but the client's second or other language. A manager, reflecting back on the impact of the training one year later, said that she had started to look at linguistic sensitivity within her team to ensure better equity in service provision:

For me, I find a growing confidence in working with clients with whom English may not be their first language. I start to look for

this awareness and skills in my counselling staff team now and
would highly recommend this training to anyone working in any
area where the community is ethnically diverse. Therapy should
not always be about white, middle-class people; we need to
ensure access to therapy for all.

The three-word limit also helps participants to focus on the age they feel
when their vocabulary is so restricted. Many participants report feeling
about three years old. This connects with the embodied experiences
of rage and fear that they experience in the carer role in this training
exercise. And these embodied experiences link to the concept of
language embodiment (Pavlenko, 2012; Caldwell-Harris, 2014), where
a client may feel one of their languages in a specific part of the body, or
may hear a word in one language that provokes a visceral reaction. Some
participants share that they can identify with the carer's experiences in the
vignette, either from their own experiences as new arrivals in the UK with
limited spoken English or on trips abroad to countries where they have
limited ability to speak the language. Other suggestions include thinking
with clients about the ages they feel in their different languages and how
this knowledge can be put to therapeutic use. Almost all participants say
that they have never thought about language and emotional age in this
way before, or that agency and power to act in the world are enabled by
complex linguistic systems. A speech and language therapist fed back
that, after this exercise, she became aware of and appreciated for the
first time the depth of loss of agency experienced by people who have
suffered aphasia after a stroke, despite all the compensatory non-verbal
communication techniques they are being taught.

As psychological therapists, how tempting it is to think that we
would never be so lacking in empathy that we would be too busy
looking at a client's 'falling' to pay attention to what they are saying.

However, we can be distracted, without realising it, by the
unfamiliar and the hard to understand, and our anxieties can narrow
the focus of the attention we are able to give to what someone is saying.
This can happen to monolingual therapists, and it can happen to
multilingual therapists too.

Identity

We are all subject to unconscious bias, which evolves from our
socialisation and our exposure to other people's preferences.

This can lead us to act on our unconscious preferences and make assumptions.

The very idea of our unconscious bias can cause anxiety. If the training context is safe, then this dark area of the self can be explored freely and lightly so that our biases can emerge and be worked with productively. As our fear of our unconscious drivers decreases, our ability to stay empathically engaged with the client is increased. The following quotation from a training participant illustrates the need, in offering empathy, to be aware of one's own bias as well as the client's perspective, by '… enabling a person to make sense of their experience in their own terms, not in my terms, [gaining] a better understanding of the patient's perspective'. Although this is, of course, necessary in all therapeutic encounters, therapy across languages and cultures places perspective-taking under an even stronger spotlight. We may want to broaden our notion of empathy and approach clients with 'wide-angle empathy' (Hawkins & Ryde, 2020), as the following case example illustrates.

Exercise 2: Talk about the talking

Aim: to help participants to experience 'live' the sense of disempowerment and loss of clinical authority when their intervention about culture or language is received negatively by a client.

The trainer explains the background to the exercise. Leila is an Iranian refugee whose first language is Farsi and who speaks quite good English as her second language. She is having counselling with an English-speaking counsellor, using English as the lingua franca. Leila sometimes finds it difficult to express herself in English in the sessions and the counsellor wonders if an interpreter might be helpful. The counsellor suggests to Leila that they could try a session with an interpreter. The trainer then takes the 'hot seat' as Leila and the rest of the group are collectively given the role of the counsellor. Leila becomes angry at the suggestion that it would be helpful to work with an interpreter. The group, as the counsellor, tries to offer interventions and the 'client' responds as she thinks appropriate.

Participants respond and react to this exercise in various ways. Some immediately back down before Leila's anger and apologise to her for possibly offending her. They suggest that they ignore their suggestion (as counsellor) and continue with the session. When Leila has continued to be angry, they have felt disempowered, lacking in authority, and sometimes guilty for not understanding why their suggestion has provoked such a strong reaction. Some groups try to encourage Leila to explain her misgivings about an interpreter. These include issues of trust in the professional abilities of the interpreter. Others focus on the technical aspects of the linguistic misunderstandings. Sometimes groups move beyond the issue with the interpreter. They explore whether Leila might feel humiliated because she believes that her English is not good enough, or may be offended because she has, in fact, spent a long time studying English and the counsellor seems to be suggesting her English is not good enough. It's also been suggested that Leila might feel she is 'too much' for the counsellor: 'That is why the counsellor wants to bring the interpreter in, because she can't cope with me on her own.' Or maybe Leila has constructed a new identity in English that she does not want to relinquish.

This exercise can also help trainees to build their confidence to repair ruptures, which inevitably occur in these sensitive contexts, and to find ways to keep connected with the client and to keep thinking. The exercise may elicit feelings such as guilt and inadequacy on the part of the counsellor. These feelings can be powerful pulls away from the professional stance of counsellor or therapist. Participants have fed back that the ability to experience those pulls in training helps them to feel more ready to respond to them in their practice:

> I feel more able to respond rather than to react defensively. I feel more confident to stay with the unknown in the room.

The exercise raises the issues of identity and language attrition and attachment. Leila may have tried to lose her first language because of the associations it has for her. As we have already seen in Chapter 1, Sarah didn't want to speak Czech any more and she had created a new identity for herself in English. Leila may associate Farsi with her past – there may have been trauma associated with her life in Iran and her home language – and English may represent her present and her future. Szekacs-Weisz notes that therapy can be experienced as constraining if 'patients (can) feel that therapy in their native language binds them in a position they want to move away from' (2004: 27). Torture survivors, interviewed about the languages of pain, survival and healing, relate that their mother tongue can feel like an oppressor and that a later learned language can provide a sense of safety (Cook, 2020):

> The English language is my place of safety. It is from that place of
> safety that I can visit my pain.

Participants are often struck by the significance of clients'
multilingualism in the development of their identity: 'Language can
help us to express a… different part of our personality.' Although Leila
did not want to speak in her first language in therapy, this actually
encourages some trainees to think for themselves and for their clients
about what not speaking a language has meant in their families and
whether some languages have been lost to them completely (Schmid,
2013) and how that has affected them:

> … and now I am wondering, thinking about how French is my
> mother tongue, my dad is from Belgium [and] my mum's from
> Switzerland, from the German-speaking part, but I was never
> fluent in German.

Participants' ideas about how they would apply the ideas and experiences
from the training exercise to their practice include addressing with
clients their linguistic repertoires as a potential therapeutic asset. I see
them begin to relate to their clients not only with general empathy but
also with a more targeted linguistic empathy:

> I am going to be more open and transparent with my clients. I am
> going to name potential barriers in our communication process
> itself. I will talk about the talking. I am going to do that with my
> clients and also with an interpreter, when I use one.

Although this exercise focuses on a client who wants to continue their
therapy in their second language, discussions about the case example
of Sarah, from Chapter 1, are often participants' first opportunity to
think about the impact of *not* inviting a client's first language into
therapy. They begin to consider how this might limit access to the
client's world. Many of the training participants have only ever thought
about the technical aspects of spoken languages – the capacity a client
has to understand or to make themselves understood – when deciding
whether to work with an interpreter. Their increased ability to tolerate
ambiguity and not understanding means that they can let go of the
technical focus. They can attend to the process and to the relational

aspects of multilingualism in therapy. They can consider how a person might bring different aspects of the self to therapy, depending on the languages they choose to speak.

Some participants begin to think with linguistic empathy about their own identities: 'I'm not a monolingual person… I'm thinking, my brain doesn't work in one language exclusively.' Trainees also consider the value of inviting all the client's languages into the room and whether this could help the client integrate different aspects of their self. One participant said of a current client:

> Does she feel like an intellectual in Russian, emotional in Italian and playful in English? How do these different aspects of herself knit up together across the different languages? I think we could explore this creatively in the therapy room.

Another participant reflected on why she hadn't considered using her first language in therapy:

> I just never considered the impact of language [and] I thought my English was good enough to do therapy. I never thought I would be better understood in [my native language], it didn't cross my mind.

In fact, research shows us that speakers of English as an additional language may find their English is too good. They may attribute greater emotionality to experiences than do their peers for whom English is their mother tongue. An explanation for this is that second language speakers may overcompensate for the emotional detachment effect of their second language (Mavrou & Dewaele, 2020).

By the end of the exercise, participants also find that they feel much less anxious about inviting clients' different languages into the room. They become aware of the potentially highly charged emotional experience for clients of talking in one or other of their multiple languages, particularly where a traumatic incident or incidents has been experienced in one of them. They think about how they can work with clients' languages in a safe way. They devise ways to invite the different languages into the room by, for example, suggesting that a client try imagining they are saying something sensitive in each of their different languages: 'I ask the client to imagine what it would feel like speaking her languages in the room, in my presence.' In this way, counsellors can empower the client to take control of their own emotional/linguistic thermostat.

Participants have also suggested asking the client to be their own interpreter, back-translating for the therapist, so that the therapist can be included in their narrative. Other very practical ideas for working with multilingualism as an asset include using a physical dictionary (not just Google Translate) as a shared object between the therapist and the client. The fact that the therapist has made the effort to obtain the dictionary can symbolise an act of care and demonstrate that they value the linguistic repertoire of the client. The dictionary is also a means to negotiate meaning and create understanding between the two people in the room. The idea of something as concrete as a dictionary emerges from the multilingual therapeutic frame that participants are beginning to apply.

Training to work collaboratively with interpreters

In this section, I want us to think about the training therapists need to be able to work with three people in the room. In Chapter 3, we considered in some depth the issues for interpreter-mediated therapy and counselling. The aim of this training intervention is to build counsellors' and therapists' confidence to work collaboratively with interpreters in counselling and therapy. Costa and Briggs (2014) researched the experiences of clients who had received interpreter-mediated therapy. The training in working collaboratively with interpreters in therapy and counselling is based on and developed from the findings from this research. The framework for the training programme is described in detail in Costa (2017b).

The training programme develops therapists' core skills in managing triadic communication; building a collaborative working relationship with the interpreter; sharing working methods and needs; exploring the experience of being in triangular relationships, and the challenges and methods of managing exclusions and collusions. The curriculum is structured around a consideration of the key issues of power and safety, exploring therapists' own relationships with power and authority and the appropriate use of their authority. These skills are necessary for therapy and counselling with clients generally, not just for interpreter-mediated therapy.

The training includes demonstrations of triadic working; some solutions for common problems; the co-creation of a list of tips for effective working and the pre-meeting with the interpreter, and relevant research findings. This is an opportunity for participants to consider the anxieties that the client, interpreter and therapist all bring to the encounter. Film clips of interpreted sessions and drama-based exercises are used to explore power dynamics in interpreter-mediated therapy.

At the beginning of a training session on working effectively with interpreters, therapists and counsellors often feel very like the participant who said in their feedback: 'At first, you know, when I first got into the weekend, I thought, "Ahhh, a whole day of working with interpreters… Hmmm, not interested, thank you very much". However, by the end of the session, she 'did change my mind completely.'

The training methodology is rooted in Action Methods (Baim, 2014; Costa, 2016), which seems to contribute to a positive outcome, judging by the evaluations. The method aims to create a safe environment where mistakes can be made and learned from. Some of the exercises described in this chapter use enactments, hot-seating and other dramatic techniques to focus trainees' attention on the practicalities and the importance of advance preparation to avoid unnecessary complications. Participants comment that the experiential method helps them feel more empowered and in control of the session. The first exercise described below can help participants to locate their anxieties about maintaining their clinical authority within an interpreter-mediated session, forming a rapport with the client and creating a safe and transparent space for all.

Trust, power, safety

It is relatively easy to focus on the technical aspects of interpreter-mediated therapy. But participants can often begin the session unaware of the relational and dynamic complexities of working in this way. An exercise like the one below can help them get in touch with the strong feelings that this work can elicit.

Exercise 3: Sharing the power

Aim: For participants to experience the feeling of losing control in an interpreter-mediated therapy session and to discover ways of keeping the control.

A demonstration is set up with three chairs in a triangle at the front of the room. Volunteers sit in the chairs, taking the roles of the client, therapist and interpreter. The trainer feeds each of them their lines until a dilemma is reached.

Counsellor (to client): I want you to know that whatever you say in this session is confidential.

Interpreter (to client): I want you to know that whatever you say in this session is confidential.

Client (to interpreter): What do you think? Can I trust her (indicates the counsellor)? Why can't I just speak to you? I trust you.

Dilemma – should the interpreter answer the client who has asked her if she can trust the therapist, or should she translate this directly back to the therapist?

The participants freeze and the audience is asked to comment and to discuss. One option is tried out and discussed: the interpreter quickly reassures the client in their own language and explains that she will have to interpret everything to the therapist. But the therapist feels excluded; the interpreter is behaving with professional competence, but the therapist doesn't know that as she doesn't understand what the interpreter is saying to the client. A second option is tried.

Interpreter (to counsellor): What do you think? Can I trust her? Why can't I just speak to you? I trust you.

Counsellor (responds to client): Of course you can trust me.

Interpreter (to client): Of course you can trust me.

Client (to interpreter): What did you have to go and tell her that for?

The client feels let down when the interpreter repeats to the therapist what she asked her. The client thought she could have a private conversation with the interpreter, without it being translated for the therapist. This leads to a discussion about power and transparency, and the therapist, client and interpreter agree to set ethical ground rules.

In the discussion after the exercise, participants comment on how quickly they, as the therapist, can lose control of the situation.

Unwittingly, they can find themselves occupying the passive position on the active-passive continuum, having allowed the session to begin without paying attention to the specific requirements of the therapeutic interpreter-mediated frame. Not understanding what is being said can make a therapist feel so disempowered that they 'forget' how to stay active in a session. Frequently therapists notice that they 'wake up' to their responsibility part-way through a session, when it may be difficult to regain their therapeutic position.

To make matters worse, therapists are almost never aware that interpreters are trained to establish the ground rules of the communication in a session. This can create difficulties for a therapist who, like the one in the above example, did not set down the ground rules, and then later attempts to do so. Communication is generally regarded by therapists as their area of expertise. Immediately there is a conflict between the two professionals in terms of professional identity and power. As far as the therapist is concerned, if they are to stay active and maintain the clinical responsibility for the session, they need to set the ground rules. But how will an interpreter feel about that?

During the exercise, most participants mention that they have never considered the concerns and anxieties an interpreter might bring to the encounter, or the specific needs they might have in order to carry out their role effectively. As one participant said, about the interpreter's own sense of anxiety and disempowerment: 'The interpreter might also feel de-skilled being in the room with a therapist.'

Participants refer to their own personal experience with authority and how this impacts on their ability to hold their clinical authority. This ability is tested when working with a third person – the interpreter – in the room. How do you balance the tension between holding your therapeutic authority and containing your own anxieties?

> When you have another person and that person is holding the power of the translation, for the therapist it's quite challenging because you feel probably a lot of time disempowered.

And do you remember the interpreter's observation from Chapter 3? 'Working in this way doesn't come naturally [to therapists] and it almost feels as if they have lost some of their power'? The challenges from the training seem to help participant therapists feel more skilled to stay active, manage the procedure and use their clinical authority appropriately.

Participants take away two sets of practical tips from this exercise. The first relates to the pre-meeting with the interpreter before the session with the client. The pre-meeting is an opportunity to discuss together aspects of your working methods. Participants can be surprised by what they learn:

> … how important it is to have time and space before the session to talk with the interpreter about the work we're going to be doing and then afterwards to debrief… I [now] prepare the interpreter for what I'm going to do, have photocopies of everything I'm going to give the client, possibly even scan them and email them to them beforehand so that they can prepare before they come.

If we don't spend time explaining to the interpreter our working methods and professional needs and finding out about theirs, we not only exclude and ignore ourselves but we also ignore the interpreter. As I mentioned in Chapter 3, an interpreter is trained to keep the communication flowing. For example, interpreters may see it as their job to comfort a crying client or to help a client to fill a silence, and this is what they will attempt to do unless we have explained to them our therapeutic rationale for sitting with distress and silence. From their perspective, an interpreter can help us understand the linguistic challenges they face – metaphors and abstract concepts (arguably, the language of therapy) do not translate easily. In this way, interpreters and therapists can start to build trust in each other's competence. The pre-briefing is a chance for therapists and interpreters to share their working methods and professional needs and requirements with each other, in order to work as a collaborative team (Costa, 2017a).

To help participants put this into practice, I ask participants to individually note down three points that they would include in a pre-meeting with an interpreter and then together to create three top tips for working effectively with an interpreter.

We then work on a second set of tips that refer to ground rules. Everyone in the room needs to own the rules of communication. In fact, rather than a set of tips, there is really only one vital rule:

Everything everybody says in the room will be translated out loud.

This should be said at the very beginning of the session. It is also important to check that the client agrees to the ground rule and to invite them to share any concerns about it. I encourage training participants to take the client's perspective. As we saw in the exercise above, unless the ground rule is explicitly stated, a client might expect to be able to have a private conversation with the interpreter that excludes the therapist. The client may say something that they do not want the therapist to hear. For everyone to share the power in the room, everyone needs to agree to follow the rule and ensure that it is established from the very beginning.

In interpreter-mediated therapy, advance planning is a useful rule of thumb: prevention rather than cure. I often model saying the ground rule: '*Everything everybody says in the room will be translated out loud,*' and I emphasise it with a circular arm movement. It can take participants a while to realise why I am doing this. By using a non-verbal signal, I am trying to set the scene for us to co-create our own shared language in the room. Having a shared signal means that we can remind each other if any pair accidentally slips into a conversation without it being translated for the third person. It is an example of sharing the power and also of using one's authority lightly and playfully.

Triangular relationships

The following exercise explores participants' experiences of triangular relationships; their anxieties about exclusion and belonging, and their compensatory, defensive and coping strategies for managing the anxieties.

Exercise 4: the Drama Triangle

Aim: to demonstrate that personal awareness of our own vulnerabilities and sensitivities in triangular relationships is important if we want to avoid replaying unhelpful dynamics between the three participants.

I invite participants to consider the triangular relationships they have experienced personally in the course of their lives, from their earliest memories. (I remind them to be aware of their own care needs and not to take part if they would prefer not to.) I ask them to think about the patterns of inclusion and exclusion at play. What coping strategies have they developed to help them manage the anxieties that triangular relationships can evoke? I warn them to share only their coping strategies, not the details of their relationships.

Some training participants describe their anxieties about being judged in a triangular relationship and how that relates to interpreter-mediated therapy:

> Maybe an interpreter would sit in the room and think that what I was doing was rubbish. Maybe they wouldn't understand it. Maybe they would think I wasn't being kind or helpful enough.

Participants discuss coping strategies for managing triangular relationships in all aspects of life. They include withdrawal, trying to keep the peace and competing for attention. We also consider the potential impact of these unconscious coping methods on the interpreter-mediated triad. This resonates with the experiences of therapists interviewed in Miller et al (2005), who talk about getting into competitive relationships with interpreters.

By the end of the training, participants feel able to take the perspective of each of the three roles in the interpreting triad – client, interpreter and therapist:

> I think the most significant impact of the training was recognising that we work as an equal threesome, that the interpreter isn't just there as a tool to be used but that we need to open the work as a triangle.

Conclusion

The two training programmes described in this chapter are designed to raise awareness of the significance of clients' multilingualism in psychological therapies. They prompt participants to start to consider their work with clients through the multilingual therapeutic frame. The training also provides a space where participants can discuss, explore and resolve some of their concerns about working with interpreters. Feedback from participants indicates that many do not realise they need the training until they have embarked on it. It confirms that there is a big gap in core therapy training with respect to multilingualism. In our increasingly multicultural, multilingual world, counsellors and therapists need to be confident in working with multilingual clients and with interpreters, if they are to provide an equitable service to their community and for equal outcomes in healthcare to become more achievable.

One other point to note is that the training aims to bracket off multilingualism as a distinct phenomenon. In their feedback, participants say that they value the chance to dedicate attention purely to multilingualism as a separate phenomenon. They are aware that language is part of the larger construct of culture and they feel better equipped to think about the specific features of language and multilingualism.

Participants say that they feel more confident, empowered and enthusiastic about working with interpreters. They feel more skilled to manage the procedure and to use their clinical authority appropriately. Most participants have not considered the potential of moral injury and vicarious trauma for interpreters and the support they might need:

> … it [the role play] gave us an understanding of what it's actually like, to take the first impact of what's said.

In the next chapter I will consider the supervision and support needs of interpreters who work in a therapeutic context. I will also consider culturally and linguistically sensitive supervision models for therapists and counsellors and the training needs of supervisors.

References

BACP, BPC, UKCP (2018). *ScoPEd: a draft framework for the education and practice of counselling and psychotherapy*. Lutterworth: BACP. www.bacp.co.uk/media/5161/scoped-competency-framework.pdf (accessed 20 June 2020).

Bager-Charleson S, Dewaele J-M, Costa B, Kasap Z (2017). A multilingual outlook: can awareness-raising about multilingualism affect therapists' practice? A mixed-method evaluation. *Language and Psychoanalysis* 6(2): 56–75.

Baim C (2014). Integrating psychodrama with attachment theory: implications for practice. In: Farrall M, Holmes P, Kirk K (eds). *Empowering Therapeutic Practice: integrating psychodrama into other therapies*. London: Jessica Kingsley Publishing (pp125–156).

Boyles J, Talbot N (2017). *Working with Interpreters in Psychological Therapy*. London: Routledge.

Bulawayo NV (2013). *We Need New Names*. London: Chatto & Windus.

Caldwell-Harris CL (2014). Emotionality differences between a native and foreign language: implications for context-dependence and embodiment. *Frontiers in Psychology: language sciences*; 30 March. https://bu.academia.edu/CatherineCaldwellHarris/ (accessed 15 June 2020).

Cook S (2020). *The impact and functions of a later learned language on survivors of torture in the context of a therapeutic community*. Unpublished PhD dissertation. London: Birkbeck, University of London.

Costa B (2017a). The strength and the stress of triangles: support and supervision for interpreters and therapists. In: Boyles J (ed). *Psychological Therapy for Survivors of Torture: a human rights approach with people seeking asylum*. Monmouth: PCCS Books (pp331–350).

Costa B (2017b). Team effort – training therapists to work with interpreters as a collaborative team. *International Journal for the Advancement of Counselling* 39(1): 1–14.

Costa B (2016) Roles in triangles: the interpreter, the client and the therapist. *The Psychotherapist* 64: 18–19.

Costa B (2011). Managing the demands of mental health interpreting: why training, supervision and support are not luxuries. *ITI Bulletin* March–April.

Costa B, Briggs S (2014). Service-users' experiences of interpreters in psychological therapy: a pilot study. *International Journal of Migration, Health and Social Care* 10(4): 231–244.

Costa B, Dewaele J-M (2019). The talking cure – building the core skills and the confidence of counsellors and psychotherapists to work effectively with multilingual patients through training and supervision. *Counselling and Psychotherapy Research* 19: 231–240.

Dewaele J-M (2016). Why do so many bi- and multilinguals feel different when switching languages? *International Journal of Multilingualism* 13: 92–105.

Dewaele J-M (2013). *Emotions in Multiple Languages* (2nd ed). Basingstoke: Palgrave Macmillan

Hawkins P, Ryde J (2020). *Integrative Psychotherapy in Theory and Practice: a relational, systemic and ecological approach*. London: Jessica Kingsley Publishing.

Mavrou I, Dewaele J-M (2020). Emotionality and pleasantness of mixed-emotion stimuli: the role of language, modality, and emotional intelligence. [Online.] *International Journal of Applied Linguistics*; 28 January. https://doi.org/10.1111/ijal.12285 (accessed 20 June 2020).

Miller E, Martell ZL, Pazdirek L, Caruth M, Lopez D (2005). The role of interpreters in psychotherapy with refugees: an explanatory study. *The American Journal of Orthopsychiatry* 75(1): 27–39.

Panicacci A, Dewaele J-M (2017). 'A voice from elsewhere': migration, personality and multiple selves in multiple languages. *International Journal of Multilingualism* 14(4): 419–436.

Pavlenko A (2012). Affective processing in bilingual speakers: disembodied cognition? *International Journal of Psychology* 47(6): 405–428.

Salaets H, Balogh K (2015). Co-Minor-IN/QUEST Research Findings. In: Balogh K, Salaets H (eds). *Children and Justice: overcoming language barriers. Cooperation in interpreter-mediated questioning of minors.* Cambridge/Antwerp/Portland: Intersentia (pp175–326).

Schmid MS (2013). First language attrition. *WIREs Cognitive Science* 4(2): 117–123.

Schrauf RW (2000). Bilingual autobiographical memory: experimental studies and clinical cases. *Culture and Psychology* 6: 387–417.

Szekacs-Weisz J (2004). How to be a bi-lingual psychotherapist. In: Szekacs-Weisz J, Ward W (eds). *Lost Childhood and the Language of Exile.* London: Imago East West (pp21–28).

Tehrani N, Vaughan S (2009). Lost in translation: using bilingual differences to increase emotional mastery following bullying. *Counselling and Psychotherapy* 9(1):11-17.

Tribe R, Thompson K (2009). Exploring the three-way relationship in therapeutic work with interpreters. *International Journal of Migration* 5(2): 13–21.

5

Linguistically sensitive
clinical supervision

This chapter addresses the need for specifically targeted supervision in the development of linguistically sensitive counselling and therapy practitioners. As I've noted, most therapists will have received little or no training in multilingualism and therapy in their core course. Anne Power titled her article about culture (2016), 'Can supervision foster the personal cultural awareness that trainings often miss out? My aspirations as a psychotherapy supervisor'; it could equally well apply to multilingualism, in my view.

But even if a therapist has had some training, they need to be continually developing their professional capability to work with linguistic sensitivity. It is, of course, important for cultural and linguistic issues to be addressed as part of the process throughout all supervision. Again, this is recognised with reference to culture more widely: 'Rather than split these off by saying "Now let's think about cultural issues", they are threaded throughout the supervision' (Ryde, 2011: 150).

Linguistic issues can too easily get overlooked in the midst of other clinical discussions. For this reason, I argue that organisations working in areas with significant multilingual populations should arrange dedicated linguistically (and culturally) sensitive supervision sessions at regular intervals – say quarterly – in order to focus practitioners' attention on these issues and remind them of the need to work within a multilingual therapeutic frame. We have already noted that multilingualism understandably provokes anxiety in some therapists and counsellors, for a range of reasons. It is difficult to work creatively when you are anxious. One of the functions of supervision is to enhance quality and creativity (BACP, 2018). It does this by providing a safe space – one that is as shame-free as possible (Costa, 2017), where uncomfortable reflexivity (Pillow, 2003) and transformative learning can take place.

In my experience, group supervision is an ideal format for this. People can express their own and hear each other's anxieties and gain encouragement to be bold and take a step onto unfamiliar terrain. Experienced supervisors will be aware of the skills needed to run supervision groups. This chapter draws out some of the additional perspectives that can be helpful when viewing case work through the multilingual frame. I offer examples of three types of supervision groups and one training intervention for clinical supervisors. The three groups serve three distinct groups of supervisees: interpreters; therapists and counsellors (monolingual and multilingual) working with multilingual clients, and multilingual therapists and counsellors. We will begin by considering supervision groups for interpreters working in therapeutic settings.

Supervision groups for interpreters working with counselling and psychotherapy clients

The support needs of sign language interpreters are increasingly recognised (ASLIA, 2011; Hetherington, 2012). So why are spoken-language interpreters' support needs not similarly recognised and served? It is recognised, however, that interpreters in mental health contexts can be emotionally disturbed and impacted negatively by the work (Doherty, MacIntyre & Wyne, 2010; Hlavac, 2017). Chapter 3 reviewed the role of interpreters in a therapeutic context, including the views of interpreters about the stresses and challenges of their work. I also referred there to a model of supervision for interpreters, and this is what I am going to consider now. This model has three functions: reparative, reflexive and responsive, which I will address in turn.

The reparative function

The reparative function combines features of professional and pastoral mentoring, which aim 'to help and support people to manage their own learning in order that they may maximise their potential, develop their skills, improve their performance and enable them to become the person they want to be' (Parsloe & Wray, 2000: 22).

The following is an example of the kind of material that interpreters might bring to a supervision group and for which this type of reparative function is suitable.

Case example

An interpreter shares with the group that she interpreted for an assessment session with a 10-year-old boy who had been referred for counselling. During the session, it emerged that the boy had recently made a suicide attempt. The interpreter believes she was able to continue to function appropriately in the session. But since the session she has been unable to stop thinking about the boy and wondering what is going to happen to him. She thinks the boy has been referred to another service. During the session, we listen to her and ask her what she needs from the group. She asks to hear from other people in the group who may have had related experiences and the coping strategies they have used to help them to continue to work with such vulnerable clients. The group participants share their experiences, and the supervisor ensures that they do not judge the interpreter who has brought the story or offer unwanted advice. At the end of the session, the participants say that they all appreciate the space to listen and share about how the work affects them so that they can stay robust and resilient enough to continue to do this type of work. Some comment on the importance of not feeling you are alone and knowing that your professional colleagues have similar dilemmas and that they are also impacted by the work.

This story from a supervision group, which is included in the anthology *In More Words* (Dillsworth & Costa, 2017), is an example of the reparative function of supervision for interpreters. This function is, of course, an aspect of all clinical supervision. For interpreters, though, the reparative function plays an important part in helping to create links and reduce isolation. Isolation is an occupational hazard for interpreters, most of whom work on a freelance basis and have few opportunities to meet up with colleagues specialising in this field. For this reason, supervision offered in groups, rather than on a one-to-one basis, can be a preferred option.

The reflexive function

The reflexive function is the one that probably has most in common with clinical supervision for counsellors and therapists. The following example illustrates how an interpreter's experience can be explored reflexively in group supervision.

Case example

An interpreter, Mia, recounts in the supervision group that she was booked for a counselling appointment but recognised the name of the client and realised she had interpreted for her before. The counsellor who booked the appointment had allowed extra time for a briefing session before the appointment began. During the pre-briefing session, in line with her training, which encourages transparency, Mia told the counsellor that she had already interpreted for the client in some sessions with social services.

The counsellor decided to go ahead with the session. At the end, the counsellor accompanied the client out of the room and checked that she was OK with Mia as the interpreter. The client said she was.

However, when Mia arrived for the next session, she saw that there was another interpreter already in the waiting room. The counsellor arrived and was very apologetic. She took Mia into another room and explained that her own clinical supervisor had advised her to book a different interpreter, one who had not worked with the client before, for the next session. The counsellor had forgotten to cancel the appointment with Mia.

Mia explains to the group that she has a number of conflicted feelings. On the one hand, she understands that it might be more boundaried to have an interpreter who does not have any prior involvement with a client. On the other hand, the counsellor had checked with the client and the client was OK with her as their interpreter. She wonders: 'What is the agency I work for going to think about the fact that the counsellor wants a different interpreter? What if I meet this client again in another context and she asks why I stopped interpreting for her?' Mia is also concerned about how the client feels about the change of interpreter. 'I am beginning to think that it is not a good idea to be transparent about my experiences with the counsellor/therapist. I thought that being honest with each other would promote a collaborative relationship, not terminate it!'

In the ensuing discussion, supervision group members highlight the limited power of interpreters, not just in terms of their working conditions but more in relation to the role they are perceived to have in the working relationship with the counsellor. They have little power and autonomy to make choices in the professional encounter (low decision latitude), which puts them at risk of stress-related burnout (Dean & Pollard, 2001: 12). In this case, the counsellor and the counsellor's supervisor had clearly had some training; they knew enough to ensure the counsellor set up a pre-briefing session and they were sensitive to the potential impact of the interpreter on the therapeutic relationship between the counsellor and the client. However, neither thought there might be a need to talk with Mia about her role and her ability for containment. Nor did it appear that the client's feelings and preferences were taken into account – although Mia didn't know for sure that this was the case. One thing was clear– no one thought to inform Mia about the decision to change interpreters.

One of the functions of reflexive supervision is to provide a safe space for interpreters to vent their feelings and to hear from others about similar experiences. It can also provide an opportunity to reflect on ways in which an interpreter might be able to re-empower herself. But there is a limit to what an interpreter can do. Low decision latitude goes with the role. After speaking and hearing from others in the group, Mia acknowledges the shared frustrations and the limits of power attached to the role of interpreter. Without this opportunity, it is possible that Mia could act out her frustrations the next time she finds herself in a situation like this.

Reflexive supervision also helps interpreters with ethical decision-making. Mia came to the group session feeling that it would be better not to be transparent about any prior relationships with clients, because of this counsellor's reaction. By the end of the group session, Mia feels she is able to connect back with her decision-making capacity and own responsibility for the decisions she can make. Despite her frustration with her minimal power in this relationship, she is able to renew her commitment to transparency.

Ethical decision-making can be a lonely process and the reflective function of the supervision group plays an important role in helping Mia feel she is not so alone.

The responsive function

The responsive function supports interpreters' exploration of systemic and organisational change. Interpreters are often considered to have only a peripheral role in organisations and systems. And yet, paradoxically, their inclusion can shed new light on existing problems

– or, indeed, create new problems. However, as illustrated above, when interpreters experience existing or new systemic problems, they have no mechanism for feeding back about them or for effecting change.

The following example from a supervision group describes an organisational problem and the responsive solution-finding function that supervision of interpreters can play.

Case example

Salma, an interpreter, has been booked to interpret for a counselling client of an NHS mental health service. Salma arrives early for the pre-briefing meeting with the counsellor. It is their second session together. When the interpreter arrives, the receptionist tells her to sit in the waiting room and points to a seat next to the client, who has also arrived early for the appointment. The interpreter asks the receptionist if she can wait somewhere else, not with the client, and the receptionist replies crossly that she can wait in the waiting room 'like all the other interpreters'.

The supervision group discussion focuses first on the power dynamics: there is a limit to the interpreter's ability to make her own decisions about where she waits for the session to begin. I am talking about low decision latitude again.

However, this NHS trust has a code of practice for working with interpreters, which includes ensuring a separate waiting area for them. Encouraged by this, Salma takes a copy of the code to her next pre-briefing session with this counsellor and asks if the counsellor can talk to the receptionist about the need for a separate waiting area for interpreters. The counsellor is reluctant as she doesn't feel this is within her brief.

In this case, there is an argument for the interpreter's supervisor or her agency to take this up with the trust. One outcome could be that suitable training might then be offered to receptionists. This is, of course, a more active response than is usual for a clinical supervisor. However, it does reflect the seventh eye of Hawkins and Shohet's (2006) seven-eyed model of supervision – the meta-organisational perspective. The responsive function of supervision for interpreters sometimes requires the supervisor to be active. (We have already considered in Chapter 3 how important it is for the therapist to stay active in interpreter-mediated therapy.) This more interventionist aspect is justified because of interpreters' low decision latitude. A supervisor who limits themselves to encouraging the interpreter to take action may not be giving enough acknowledgement to the limited authority an interpreter has to make necessary changes to their working conditions. It can be frustrating for an interpreter to be 'empowered' to be assertive and take action within their supervision group, yet be unable to effect actual change. If a supervisor does not understand this and is not keeping the meta-organisational perspective in mind, then an interpreter is unlikely to trust that supervision can be useful.

Supervision groups for therapists and counsellors working with multilingual clients

Supervision groups that address multilingualism in psychological therapies can provide a protected space to think about culture and language integratively and also as discreet phenomena. In common with most group supervision, the sessions are most successful when there is sharing by all: some participants bring something and others in the group connect what is shared with their own experiences. The supervisor might want to share information and offer useful models, if indicated by the case material. She may also prepare some sample case examples in order to model the multilingual focus of the group.

The teaching component in this type of supervision is mentioned because of the potential gaps in participants' initial training and lack of experience of viewing their work from within a multilingual therapeutic frame. The following two examples include one case of interpreter-mediated therapy from the therapist's perspective and two cases of working in English as a lingua franca.

Case example: interpreter-mediated session

Fran, the therapist, describes a recent session with an interpreter. At the beginning of the session, she is feeling confident and in control. She is pleased that she has had a briefing session with the interpreter before the session began with the client. When she worked with an interpreter before, she found it difficult when the client wanted to talk for a long time, hardly pausing for breath, and it was impossible for the interpreter to translate everything – there was so much! This time, she has taken the initiative and, in the pre-briefing, asks the interpreter to stop the client from time to time, so that he can interpret for her.

The session starts and the interpreter stops the client in order to translate. But things do not go according to plan. The client gets cross with the interpreter. The interpreter translates the client's words. 'Why are you stopping me when I want to get this all off my chest?'

The therapist feels that she lost control of the session at this point and she asks the group for help to think about what was going on.

With the supervisor's support, the group starts to unravel the shifting power dynamics within this session. They think about the active-passive continuum. It is crucial to pay attention to where you are, as a therapist, throughout the session, not just at the beginning. Fran began the session in the active position. She then handed over her active function – managing the communication to the interpreter.

Various members of the group share similar experiences. They find the thread begins with Fran's request to the interpreter to stop the client from time to time so that he can interpret for her. What appears to be an example of the therapist using her authority is in fact an abdication of her responsibility. When Fran handed over control of the communication flow to the interpreter, she lost her authority before the session had even started. Even if the therapist does not understand what the client is saying, she has to keep control of the communication flow. If anyone is going to stop the client, it needs be the therapist. If the client is going to get angry about that, they are more likely to direct their anger at the therapist, rather than at the interpreter.

Power dynamics in interpreter-mediated communication are very subtle, as we have seen in Chapter 3. In this situation, if the supervisor deems it appropriate, she might introduce a model such as the Drama Triangle (Karpman, 1968), to illustrate how quickly power and oppression can ebb and flow. In my experience, therapists taking part in groups and discussions such as these find that they become more confident to 'talk about the talking' – to explore with clients and interpreters the barriers and facilitators to communication and methods for negotiating and trying out different approaches.

The next two examples illustrate the dilemmas that underlie the technical solution of working in English as a lingua franca. The therapists in these two examples are open to exploring the political and the relational aspects that different languages can hold for their clients.

The first example involves a client who is a child, but much of the discussion could also apply to adult clients.

Case example: working in English as a lingua franca (1)

A child psychotherapist is working with a nine-year-old boy, Jan, who came to England from Poland with his family two years ago. The therapist has been told that Jan's English is good, but he has become increasingly withdrawn at school and has been referred for therapy. When they meet, Jan is very quiet in the session and keeps asking if he can leave. The therapist shares with the supervision group that she is not sure whether Jan can understand everything she says and if he can express himself in English. She thinks it could be a language issue but isn't sure. She asks the group to help her to think about this.

Initially, the group focuses in on the technical aspects of this case. Could the therapist ask for a formal language assessment? Should she invite an interpreter in so that she can see if it is possible to 'eliminate the language problem'? After a while, the supervisor steers the discussion onto more relational issues. She encourages the group to stay with the 'language problem' a little longer. She helps them think about the client's multilingualism not as a deficit but as a potential asset in the therapy. Is there a way, for example, that the therapist could explore with Jan the meaning and emotional costs and consequences of speaking or not speaking Polish and/or English? Is he quieter in one language than in another? Can the therapist bring both languages into the room by creative means – perhaps by using stone work, where Jan picks one stone to represent Polish and another to represent English? What would it be like for Jan to speak Polish in the room? Could he teach the therapist how to say hello and goodbye, for example? Could they have fun with the language?

I recall a participant in a different supervision group who described how she invited a Zimbabwean client to express the concept of 'over-thinking' in their first language, Shona, and together they then searched for the translation in a Shona-English dictionary.

Of course, all of these ideas may not bear fruit. But it can be useful to use the multilingual therapeutic frame to move away from the convenience of a technical solution and explore what can emerge if we dare to stay with not knowing.

Case example: working in English as a lingua franca (2)

Dev is a student on a postgraduate course of study. Dev is originally from India and coming to England to study is the fulfilment of a dream for him.

However, he has recently been told that his English is not good enough and that he will have to do an extra course in English for academic purposes. His confidence has been badly affected and he has become depressed. He decides to seek help from the university counselling service. He tells the counsellor, Alison, that he knows how important English is in order to succeed in his career and says he wishes he could speak English like her. Alison feels embarrassed and tries to equalise things between them by saying that she cannot speak any other language and that she is impressed that Dev can speak two other languages fluently besides English. But Dev says he is ashamed of his other languages and he would be happy to give them up if he could speak fluent English. Alison is feeling rather uncomfortable about this interaction and takes it to her group supervision session.

The group empathises with Alison's discomfort and then starts to talk about the political inequality of different world languages. The monolingual members of the group discuss their sense of inadequacy about their language skills and their admiration for their clients who speak more than one language. Having voiced this, they then acknowledge that bringing their own inadequacy into the conversation with a client may not be helpful (as it wasn't with Dev).

The group then goes on to discuss whether a counsellor or therapist has a role in challenging political structures. After a long discussion, Alison says she feels more confident to acknowledge in the room, with Dev, the reality of the status of English in the world. She suggests she could invite Dev to consider the prestige of the English language as a product of history rather than as an immovable fact. She recognises that Dev needs to engage with his current reality – he wants to get his qualification and he needs to do this in English – but he might be able also to consider the values that underpin this linguistic power dynamic. This might also help him to re-think his shame about his own languages and cultural heritage.

The supervisor suggests they try this out in a role play. Alison takes the role of Dev and another member of the group plays Alison. By exploring the structural power inequalities of languages in clinical supervision (and by stepping into Dev's shoes in the role play), Alison becomes more aware of the prestige of English in the world and her own relationship with her linguistic privilege. This helps her not to act out in the therapy room her own sense of inadequacy and her shame about her linguistic privilege. It also helps her to feel more confident to address the power issues embedded in the different languages she and Dev speak and to explore this further with Dev, if this is what he wants to do. Alison says that the supervision session has helped her not to react defensively and to be able to reflect with her client so that he has the option to explore the linguistic power dynamics further.

The following fragment of a scripted dialogue illustrates the role play exploring how a client might articulate their experience of linguistic privilege:

Therapist: But I really am impressed that you can speak so many languages. I mean it.

Client: You don't understand. Having an accent, and I mean a foreign accent, is like your invisible skin colour. Just like, when you walk into a room and you are brown or black, you have shown everyone your ethnic passport.

Therapist: (*Quietly*) Is it really that bad?

Client: Except this marker isn't visible. But when you open your mouth to speak, it marks you out. You could call it audio-racism.

Therapist: I didn't mean that when I said…

Client: If you have a standard British accent like you – or better still, a posh one – you can pass as someone civilised, knowledgeable, credible. It makes your skin colour more palatable.

Between 2014 and 2016, I asked counsellors and psychotherapists who attended our quarterly culturally and linguistically supervision and/or training sessions to complete an evaluation form. I used this approach to monitor the impact and quality of the supervision and training I was providing.

I asked them to rate the impact of the supervision and training, using a scoring system.

On average, there was an improvement of four points on a 10-point scale in their linguistic and cultural empathy, awareness and confidence in their own clinical authority and interest in the nature of communication. Some participants chose to make additional comments, including these:

I have a much deeper sense of empathy with clients who are culturally and linguistically different from me.

I now really try to understand the perspective and world view of another person and I am increasingly aware of my own cultural biases.

I feel able to encourage clients to use phrases or words from their native language… to gain and rebalance power within the therapeutic alliance.

I am quicker at spotting when I feel uncomfortable or uncertain in how to approach issues like the impact of the history of colonialism on languages, culture and therapy.

I feel more prepared to acknowledge my own anxiety and bias and to allow curiosity, and I feel able to stay with linguistically different clients rather than immediately referring them on to specialist services.

Although the scores and the comments were all drawn from self-reports, the fact that people felt there was an improvement would suggest that there is a value in this type of supervision session.

Supervision groups for multilingual counsellors and therapists

Supervision groups for multilingual counsellors and psychotherapists can support them to think about the particular challenges and opportunities their multilingual identities afford them when working with multilingual and monolingual clients. The aim of such groups is for multilingual therapists to become more confident in how to use their own and their clients' multilingualism as a therapeutic asset.

The groups can provide a space to think about the issues raised in Chapter 2, such as the impact of working as a multilingual therapist in a language in which you weren't trained. They also provide space to think about working in English when it's not your first language, with a client for whom English is their first language. Some of the issues that are regularly covered include the disjunction between managers' expectations and the realities of working therapeutically in multiple languages; clients' expectations; technical language issues around terms and vocabulary that do not translate easily; finding one's professional identity in one's home language; feeling a 'fraud'; the speed at which therapy can move and assumptions that can be made, and maintaining your therapeutic footing when working in a minority language with a client.

Case example

Amna is a counsellor with a voluntary sector agency. She has just started working with a couple, Mr and Mrs Shah, who have been referred on the advice of the school attended by their 12-year-old daughter, Sara. Sara's teachers have noticed that she has been self-harming and she has been referred to the school counsellor. The couple are both of Pakistani heritage. Mrs Shah came to the UK 13 years ago when she married Mr Shah, who was born and brought up in the UK. They describe themselves as very traditional. They are very angry because they feel that Sara has brought shame on the family.

They say that Sara was a good girl until she started secondary school. She used to help with the cooking and cleaning and would carry all the heavy shopping home from the market. Now she says she wants to be able to have the same freedom as her 13-year-old brother. She tells them that it is not fair that, because she is a girl, she has to do all the jobs and her brother does nothing.

Mr and Mrs Shah have been very angry with her and will not allow her to go out on her own, wear make-up, or meet up with friends. She has to do all the chores or she is punished.

Amna shares a similar cultural and linguistic heritage with the Shahs, although she is nearer to their daughter's age. They speak Punjabi in the counselling sessions. Amna feels very conflicted: her instinct is to be sympathetic towards the daughter and she cannot help feeling judgemental towards the parents. She takes the case to her supervision group as she wants their help to explore this conflict.

The group supervisor thinks that this could be an opportunity to think more widely about the issues raised by this case. She asks Amna if it would be OK if she asks some questions that everyone in the group could think about with Amna. The supervisor thinks that this could be a constructive way of approaching Amna's conflicted feelings as it would allow everyone to share their reactions and think together about a way forward. This is an example of how a supervisor might expand on the case material presented so that some training input can be included. Not only does this have an educational purpose, but it also allows the group, and Amna, some space to engage with the sensitive issues. Amna agrees to the supervisor's suggestion and so the group thinks together about the following questions:

1. What feelings come up for you, when you hear Amna's account of the session?

2. If you had to take sides, whose side would you take?

3. Can you find empathy/compassion for Sara?

4. Can you find empathy/compassion for Mr and Mrs Shah?

5. What do you think could be the barriers to your working effectively with this family?

6. What could be enablers?

7. What do you think are the key issues?

The group talks about the barriers. Group members offer the following: taking sides from cultural perspectives; thinking that a child-centred approach is culturally neutral or superior to other approaches, and thinking about the culturally relevant aspects of equality. They agree that a major enabler in this situation is to be able to hold multiple perspectives in mind. Everyone seems to understand why Amna is feeling conflicted.

The supervisor then asks the group if they think that language plays any part in Amna's conflict, as it hasn't been specifically mentioned. This gets the group talking some more. Many participants mention the additional pull to make assumptions when a language is shared, and for this shared language to emphasise the similarities between clients' and therapists' own social/family relationships. A number of participants also mention how they can find it easy to inadvertently slip out of the professional, non-judgemental role of therapist and into a more social, value-laden position when they are working in their home language. One says: 'I find myself thinking, can't you be a bit more modern in your ideas?' They discuss how the group supervision sessions help them to be more alert to the difficulty of holding the boundary when working in a shared minority language with a client. Another comments: 'When I am working in my own language with a client, I know they are expecting me to be more flexible with them – like "No one will know if you do ..."'

Some report feeling inadequate when trying to think in their home language about their therapeutic model if they trained in it in English. This echoes Kokaliari and colleagues' (2013) findings that multilingual clients can spend some time during a session translating into English their own thoughts and terms, which are more accessible to them in their home language, including early memories and culturally specific words. They assert that the cognitive process of contemporaneous translation can cause internal conflict for multilingual clients and can be similarly problematic for multilingual therapists. For some CBT techniques, therapists also find it difficult to distinguish in other languages between, for example, the terms 'worries' and 'general anxiety'.

The supervisor encourages the group to share the different strategies they have for noticing and managing these additional pressures when they are working in their home languages. One solution shared by a participant is to pre-translate educational interventions that are designed to help the client to identify thoughts, emotions, physical symptoms and behaviour so that they can take things more slowly. This strategy (on the face of it, a purely technical one) also helps them to manage another process concern of 'taking things too fast' with clients with whom they share a first language. The strategies therapists have developed to help them to translate terms and vocabulary also provide them with valuable additional thinking and reflective time with their clients, so they are better able to understand their perspectives. Some participants also mention becoming more confident about negotiating with managers around the complexity of working in this way: 'I ask my manager for extra time to write up my notes in English, when I have been speaking and listening to Polish in the session.' Another strategy mentioned is to continue reading up on multilingualism and identity.

The supervisor suggests that Amna role-plays the counselling session in the group in English, to see if that feels significantly different. Amna tries out the role-play and is not surprised to find that she is more able to keep her footing as a therapist. She says she will hold onto the memory of this as a kind of mental 'flashcard' when she next works with these clients, even though she will continue to work with them in Punjabi. At the end of the supervision session, she says that she feels that she has a clearer sense of her own identity as a multilingual therapist and feels better equipped, with a number of strategies to help her to stay in her professional role and continue thinking with Mr and Mrs Shah, instead of responding reactively to them.

Training module for clinical supervisors in linguistically sensitive supervision

At the beginning of this chapter I mentioned the title of Anne Power's (2016) article, which refers to the need for supervision to foster the cultural awareness not covered in trainings. As we have noted in previous chapters, there is a need to add linguistic awareness to that aspiration. However, the problem is that even highly experienced clinical supervisors have almost certainly not received any training in multilingualism in psychological therapies. Many supervisors can therefore feel at a loss to support their supervisees with linguistic issues. Some supervisors may not even be aware of the need to address the multilingualism of supervisees and supervisees' clients.

To respond to this gap as we experienced it at Mothertongue, I devised a specialist training programme for supervisors. Although the training is a specialist programme, it is aimed at all supervisors. The programme is a highly experiential one-day session that not only aims to help supervisors think about the issues but also provides a space for them to try out how they would implement their ideas in practice.

The training seeks to help supervisors build the confidence of their supervisees to work with cultural and linguistic sensitivity. It addresses topics such as the role of multilingualism and working collaboratively with interpreters; linguistic sensitivity in practice; unconscious linguistic bias, assumptions and privilege; owning one's cultural mistakes/clumsiness; how to repair ruptures in therapeutic relationships, and working productively with power dynamics in therapy across language.

Participants are encouraged to think about how they could introduce issues of language in supervision sessions, at the relational as well as the technical level, as another lens through which to examine case material. This may involve preparing teaching material about multilingualism in advance of sessions. Teaching input is not always expected from clinical supervision, especially when supervising experienced therapists, but its inclusion here illustrates the expertise and specific training needed by supervisors who want to address these issues.

The programme begins by considering how supervisors can make the supervisory relationship as shame-free a space as possible – somewhere that supervisees can try out new ways of thinking and working and risk making mistakes. Participants are encouraged to think about unconscious/implicit bias as a universal phenomenon that we can address productively through growing awareness and willingness to face the unknown. In the words of one course participant: 'The course points out really useful (and sometimes unexpected) aspects of supervision in culturally and linguistically different clients.'

Case material similar to the examples given earlier in this chapter is used to help supervisors to think with their supervisees about the impact of multilingualism in therapy and about the dynamics of working with an interpreter. Much of the case work is considered interactively by the group as a whole. I try to model and encourage participants to take different roles by taking the roles of supervisee, client or supervisor myself and inviting the group to take the reciprocal role to mine. For example, if I am the supervisee, the group as a whole, role-plays the supervisor.

One of the key pedagogical approaches to this training is the use of meta-questions. An example of this is to ask participants why they think I took a particular decision to respond in a certain way in a role play. After we've discussed this question, I follow up with a further question about why I asked them the original question. The purpose of the meta-questioning is to allow space for the participants to deconstruct what I am doing, analyse and evaluate its effectiveness and then reconstruct it and incorporate it into their own supervisory identity, in the way that works for them. (I have just realised that I followed the same method for writing this book!)

Also included in this training is an opportunity to consider multilingualism in relationship therapy and counselling. Because many of the cases described in this chapter are also used in the supervision training, I will use a relationship therapy example in this section of the chapter. In the example, I facilitate the discussion and the posing of meta-questions, rather than take a role in the role play.

Exercise: cross-language couples

Participating supervisors are asked to think about how they would address the following questions from a supervisee:

- What should I bear in mind when working with cross-language couples – for example where one partner speaks English as their first language and the other partner speaks another language as their first language?

- Whose language(s) do I speak in and how does that affect the dynamics in the room?

- How do I work with an interpreter and a couple?

- What happens if one member of the couple needs an interpreter and the other does not?

- What happens if it is only the therapist who does not share the language(s) of the other participants?

A case is then presented. The following is a script I have written for training purposes, from a filmed excerpt of a Skype supervision session.[1] The supervisee addresses the participants of the training directly, as if they are her collective supervisor.

Case example

There's a situation I would really welcome your help with. I have been seeing a couple with an interpreter. They are Polish. The husband speaks good English, but the wife does not, so I arranged for an interpreter. I was feeling quite confident as I have had training in working with an interpreter and I had made sure that we had a pre-meeting to establish our working methods, share some context about the clients and establish our communication ground rules. The interpreter seemed very experienced and actually the sessions had been going pretty well. But half-way through the most recent session, the husband turned to me and started to talk to me directly in English. I let it go for a while – I was trying to think about what was happening relationally with this turn in the communication. However, while I was thinking, the interpreter turned to me and asked me what he should be translating. It was a really annoying question and interfered with my thinking. I told him to translate the Polish. (I thought that would have been obvious.) So that was the first thing.

The husband continued to talk directly to me in English and I thought

---

1. The film was created with the support of the Birkbeck Wellcome Trust Institutional Strategic Support Fund.

I should address the shifting power dynamics with the wife. So, I said: 'I have noticed that sometimes your husband talks to me in English and you can't understand. I wonder what that feels like when he excludes you in that way? Does that happen a lot in your relationship?'

At this point, the wife got very cross with me and asked me if I saw him talking English to me as a bad thing. She said I was wrong, that she was very proud that her husband had learned English so quickly and that he could make himself understood with English people. He had made a big effort to learn English so that their family could benefit and could make progress here in this country. I then got very confused, and I think things just went from bad to worse. Can you help me think through what might have been happening and how I could have dealt with the rupture?

After watching the film, participating supervisors think about how they might work with a supervisee who brought this dilemma to supervision. They think about the implications of seeing the interpreter as a technical resource that can be managed with a set of rules, rather than thinking about the relationship. I ask them if they can think of a meta-question they can ask me. One participant asks: 'What was on your mind when you decided to include the confusion with the interpreter in the script?' I reply that there were two reasons. First, it was to illustrate a non-technical, more relational issue about working with an interpreter. Second, I wanted to illustrate that we can easily become complacent if we have had some training in how to work effectively with an interpreter. Even after the training, we can get caught up in all kinds of relational dynamics.

The participants then think about how to choose linguistically sensitive case material to offer supervisees for discussion in sessions that might be helpful in opening up multilingual awareness. Participants often mention that they do not routinely introduce training material into supervision sessions. This might be a cultural shift in the way in which they conduct supervision.

Returning to the scripted exercise, the participants go on to consider the impact on the therapist's confidence of being addressed in different languages and having to manage the communication flow. They speculate that maybe the therapist's anxieties about inclusion and exclusion have led her to make a hasty assumption about the way in which language is used in the couple's relationship, rather than exploring the dynamics more lightly with the couple.

None of the participants have had these issues addressed in their core training. Systemic therapy underpins a number of models of relationship counselling. It aims to address the complexity of human existence and the dynamics of power relations, but there are omissions in the model that might limit its usefulness when working with multilingual clients. For example, the systemic model of the 'social graces' (Burnham, 2012) lists areas of social difference to provide a structure to consider power, privilege, oppression and difference. The social graces currently include gender, geography, race, religion, age, ability, appearance, class, culture, ethnicity, education, employment, sexuality, sexual orientation and spirituality. They represent the beliefs, values and status that underlie people's identities and world views. However, multilingualism/languages are notably absent from the list.

Participants on the supervisor training have been asked to rank their own ability, knowledge and confidence to support supervisees' work with multilingual clients at the beginning and end of the training. Again, this is a self-report method that uses a simple scoring system. Many of the participants are experienced clinical supervisors. All the same, several have said that they started the training with a score of one or two out of 10. The average score at the end of the training has been 7.5 out of 10. The training sessions are usually only one day, so even a small input into training supervisors to work with multilingualism seems to make a difference.

Conclusion

Given that the linguistic profile of the UK population has evolved so dramatically in recent decades and since core therapy trainings were first designed, the lack of multilingual awareness among therapists and supervisors is worrying. This lack of awareness may contribute to the inequity in provision of therapy to people with limited English skills. I would argue that the case for its inclusion in core training is unquestionable. I'd also argue, based on the response to the trainings I've led, that it can be refreshing and revitalizing for counsellors and psychotherapists to look at their work from this perspective. As one participant on the supervision training said:

> It went to all the areas that I have never been able to find in
> lived detail. I felt challenged, out of my depth, enlightened,
> emboldened and curious to learn more, and have learnt to reflect

on my practice and supervisory capacity in new and unexpected ways. What I learnt on the day will have a significant impact on my work with all clients and supervisees for years to come.

References

ASLIA [Australian Sign Language Interpreters Association] (2011). *Guidelines for Interpreting in Mental Health Settings*. Parramatta, NSW: ASLIA. https://aslia.com.au/wp-content/uploads/ASLIA-Mental-Health-Guidelines.pdf (accessed 22 June 2020).

BACP (2018). *Ethical Framework for the Counselling Professions*. Lutterworth: BACP.

Burnham J (2012). Developments in Social GGRRAAACCEEESSS: visible-invisible, voiced-unvoiced. In: Krause I-B (ed). *Culture and Reflexivity in Systemic Psychotherapy: mutual perspectives*. London: Karnac (pp181–203).

Costa B (2017). The strength and the stress of triangles: support and supervision for interpreters and therapists. In: Boyles J (ed). *Psychological Therapy for Survivors of Torture: a human rights approach with people seeking asylum*. Monmouth: PCCS Books (pp331–350).

Dean RK, Pollard Jr RQ (2001). Application of demand-control theory to sign language interpreting: implications for stress and interpreter training. *Journal of Deaf Studies and Deaf Education* 6(1): 1–14.

Dillsworth E, Costa B (2017). *In More Words: first international anthology of interpreters' stories*. Reading: Mothertongue.

Doherty SM, MacIntyre AM, Wyne T (2010). How does it feel for you? The emotional impact and specific challenges of mental health interpreting. *Mental Health Review Journal* 15(3): 31–44.

Hawkins P, Shohet R (2006). *Supervision in the Helping Professions* (3rd ed). Maidenhead: Open University Press.

Hetherington A (2012). Supervision and the interpreting profession: support and accountability through reflective practice. *International Journal of Interpreter Education* 4(1): 46–57.

Hlavac J (2017). *Mental Health Interpreting Guidelines for Interpreters*. Melbourne: Monash University. https://aslia.com.au/wp-content/uploads/Monash-Mental-Health-Interpreting-Guidelines-for-Interpreters-29.XI_.2017.pdf (accessed 22 June 2020).

Karpman S (1968). Fairy tales and script drama analysis. *Transactional Analysis Bulletin* 7(26): 39-43.

Kokaliari E, Catanzarite G, Berzoff J (2013). It is called a mother tongue for a reason: a qualitative study of therapists' perspectives on bilingual psychotherapy treatment implications. *Smith College Studies in Social Work 83*: 97–118.

Parsloe E, Wray M (2000). *Coaching and Mentoring: practical methods to improve learning*. London: Kogan Page.

Pillow W (2003). Confession, catharsis, or cure? Rethinking the uses of reflexivity as methodological power in qualitative research. *International Journal of Qualitative Studies in Education* 16(2): 175–196.

Power A (2016). Can supervision foster the personal cultural awareness that trainings often miss out? My aspirations as a psychotherapy supervisor. *Journal of Psychotherapy and Counselling Psychology Reflections* 1(1): 35–40.

Ryde J (2011). Culturally sensitive supervision. In: Lago C (ed). *The Handbook of Transcultural Counselling and Psychotherapy*. Maidenhead: Open University Press (pp142–152).

6

Multilingualism in groupwork with children, adults and wider systems

An individual is part of a larger society. If I benefit, people I am connected to feel better as well. Counselling client

Therapy can help when people are in distress. You may also believe, as I do, that it is important to think about interventions that can help people when therapy may not be the best intervention. This chapter addresses some of the ways in which, with others, I have tried to develop supportive activities that will be helpful to multilingual client groups.

Inclusion and exclusion have been implicit themes throughout this book. Multilingualism creates insider and outsider groups. Not understanding what people around you are saying can feel very uncomfortable, if not actively dangerous. The debates about insider and outsider status are particularly potent in today's political situation, both globally and here, in the UK. Groupwork can be one way of engaging subtly with these issues. Therapy services staffed by counsellors and psychotherapists who are trained in models of therapy that prize individual autonomy and independence can sometimes find the collective approach a challenge. The dyadic relationship can be prioritised over other forms of relating. There are a variety of possible impacts from prioritising this kind of relationship. People who come from more collective-centred cultures and family systems may be more used to and more comfortable with group interactions and may not engage with the dyadic relational intimacy of counselling and therapy. They may be more familiar with the fluctuations of multiple relationships across the lifecycle, with family and community members moving in and out of dependency, independence and interdependence with others across the generations. For some clients, their emotional issues and distress are intrinsically linked with their social situation and their sense of dislocation. Individual counselling may not be what they require; a supportive group encounter may be more relevant to their needs.

And there is at least one other possible effect when the emphasis is placed on the dyadic counselling relationship: clients can find that, when they are considering how to finish counselling or therapy, they are faced with two choices. They can finish counselling and face the immediate future without the support of the intense therapeutic relationship. Or they can try to avoid the void by continuing the counselling relationship, if they can, even when finishing counselling may be the right next step for them.

Purposive peer support and community groups can serve a very helpful function in this situation by providing a link for clients between the intimacy of the intense dyadic relationship of counselling or psychotherapy and the broader relationship with the wider community and the wider world. Groups can also draw on the participants' multilingual skills and assets. Participants who share home languages can support each other to understand and communicate in the lingua franca of the group so that those who have less mastery of the lingua franca are not excluded.

Towards the end of the previous chapter, I cited the systemic approach in relation to couple and relationship counselling and psychotherapy. In this chapter, I consider multilingualism and systems more explicitly by thinking about the role of multilingualism in groupwork with children, young people and adults. I also look further afield at the role of multilingualism in supportive activities with a wider social activist focus.

Groupwork with multilingual children: A Place to Belong

In this section I will describe a project called A Place to Belong. The project was an initiative that sought to recognise the social value that children's multilingualism brings to the school community. It aimed to provide a space where children's home languages and English were both welcome. The project consisted of a series of workshops that were delivered in six schools in the Reading area by a highly experienced community art facilitator.

It can feel very frightening and lonely to be in a new school and not know anyone or understand what is going on. When you are newly arrived in a country and you do not speak the language of the school either, it can be even more frightening and lonely. A Place to Belong offered a series of art workshops in schools for newly arrived children who did not speak English. The workshops were a place in the school where these children could feel they belonged, where they could express themselves without words and where they also had the freedom to speak in their home languages without getting into trouble. They could speak their own language and try out a new one – English – and all their expressive and linguistic skills would be valued.

The children expressed their ideas, their thoughts and feelings through visual media. Their lack of a common spoken language was not a barrier to their communication with others. The volunteer language supporters spoke Arabic, Farsi, Nepali, Portuguese, Punjabi and Spanish, which helped the children feel at ease. It made a difference to them to hear their home languages being spoken in the school environment.

The workshops provided a light-touch therapeutic intervention that helped young people to integrate different aspects of themselves via their different languages through a third medium – visual art. By using visual art, rather than words, they were able to feel they had some mastery over their communication and a sense of personal agency – a relief from the infantilising experience of trying to communicate in basic English. The workshops also provided a relaxed environment where they could experience the value of their languages, rather than being placed in a deficit position because they lacked the target language and their home language had no power or value in their new environment. Quite simply, it gave them linguistic agency.

Although the art facilitator spoke only English, and she was the only person in the group who was monolingual, she inspired the young people to create beautiful artefacts. Creating art was the overt aim of the group, but the by-products of learning English and achieving a sense of belonging in school were important and subtle secondary aims. As one pupil who participated in the groups said:

> When the group first started, I didn't know anyone, and I was a bit
> scared. But now I have friends across the year groups and really
> enjoy coming to the group.

A teacher from one of the participating schools commented on the improvement in the participating children's English:

> This morning, three girls from yesterday's group came for their
> English as an additional language lesson. As it is the end of term,
> I said they could play games (in order to draw out language). One
> became a natural leader, one used language to confirm rules and
> the third spoke more than ever before in front of me. It was all
> natural communication which reflected the confidence they are
> gaining. As this has happened only recently, I believe that the
> Place to Belong project has made a big difference for them.

Children, young people and multilingualism

Why is it important for children to maintain their home languages? I've already mentioned the possible impact of language attrition on people's psychological development (Schmid, 2013). Children as well as adults are susceptible to language attrition. It is apparently not unusual for a six-year-old internationally adopted child to lose most of her expressive native language within the first three months of moving to a new country. This is a rapid process and it is a significant loss (Gindis, 2004). Although the context for this research is international adoption, I would argue that the experience is similar for children who have moved recently to a new country and are having to learn a new language.

Not only does a child lose the facility to speak another language but they can also lose a sense of connection with their heritage, their culture of origin and their extended families:

> For children and adults, language represents more than the ability
> to communicate. It also helps a child to access and be accessed by
> groups of people who share the same language, and to reinforce
> the child's sense of their own cultural group identity. (Dutt &
> Phillips, 2000: 50)

This chimes with my own experience. I grew up in a bilingual family in the UK. But English – one of my mother's home languages – was the only language I learned. It is only as an adult that I have appreciated the loss of not learning my father's language. Passing on languages across generations is like receiving a gift from the past, looking after and using it in the present and passing it on to the future (Fishman, 1997).

Children who are proud of their multiple identities, cultures and languages are much more likely to develop resilience, greater tolerance and cognitive competence (Burck, 2005; Costa, Dioum & Yorath, 2015). It is suggested that biculturalism and multilingualism help adolescents to adapt to dual environments and minimise negative effects of acculturation (Buriel et al, 1998). There are suggested cognitive benefits, too, in being multilingual, such as improved working memory, focus and attention (Bialystok & Barac, 2013).

Groupwork with multilingual adults: the Knitting Group

Eleftheriadou (2010) likens the experience of entering a new culture to that of a baby coming into the world. She draws a parallel with the effects of the overwhelming anxiety of managing the practicalities of the new world – for example, finances and housing.

> There is a parallel with the new experience of babies and their need to sleep so much in the first three days after birth. They need more holding during this time, and then they can proceed with exploring the new environment. (2010: 121)

She also believes that the newly arrived person can 'become overwhelmed with the newness of everything around them' (2010: 121) unless they have some space that is free from these anxieties.

Isolation and loneliness can be unavoidable for people who have recently arrived in a new country. It can be hard to meet new people. Opportunities to meet in a group are often welcomed. For people who are not fluent in the language of the host country, it can be even harder to navigate this new world. It can be daunting to try to build a bridge between themselves and others – the known and the unknown. A Place to Belong was a creative task-focused group. One of the aims of the group was to create a structure on which to build bridges. With a creative, task-focused group, participants can feel like full members of a group even when they know very little of the host language. They can feel safe to choose the level of disclosure and intimacy they wish to share. A loosely defined therapy or support group may not provide sufficiently robust containment. A talking group may exclude those whose language is not the dominant language of the group.

Although language groups can be set up, there seems to be value in groups where people who would not usually meet can come together in a setting where there are no expectations of them. They are not required to perform or meet any standards of achievement; it is simply an opportunity to make connections with others and with the outside world at their own pace, in a safe, containing space (Bowlby, 1982) – one that provides 'holding during this time, and then they can proceed with exploring the new environment' (Eleftheriadou, 2010:121).

One example of such a group is the Knitting Group. This was set up as an extension of therapeutic provision within the Mothertongue counselling service. The group was a circle for women newly arrived in a small city in the UK with very few, if any, personal and social contacts. It was initially open to men, but none attended, although they did take part in other activities, such as a gardening group we established.

Some of the women attending the Knitting Group had already had a course of counselling. For them, the group provided a transitional space after the intimacy of the dyadic counselling relationship had ended, as described above. Some joined as a route into counselling – it was a chance for them to check out Mothertongue as an organisation before committing themselves. It was a space where participants could connect with others safely in a small, contained group, as a stepping-stone to connecting with the wider community.

Importantly, as well as building sustainable, supportive relationships with each other, they were able to feel they were productive contributors to the society in which they now lived by knitting and donating blankets to the premature baby unit at the local hospital. As I have noted in earlier chapters, limited fluency in a language affects your sense of agency. It could be significant for a Knitting Group member to feel she was having a positive impact on the new world in which she was living as a producer, rather than as a consumer. The knitters also explored ways in which their handiwork and skills could produce an income for their families. For example, one participant, who was a reluctant knitter to begin with, ended up designing her own patterns and selling her creations from her own website. In fact, several of the participants were initially reluctant knitters.

A meta-question of the type I included in the section on training supervisors could be handy here: 'What were some of the non-obvious intentions behind setting up the knitting group?'

The knitting was, in a way, a 'cover' for the experience and activity of the other by-products: being with other people; improving participants' English; feeling a sense of belonging; talking or not talking, and sharing with others at whatever level felt comfortable.

Bearing in mind that the adjustment period is one of great vulnerability, the group was intentionally only for newly arrived women. They had varying levels of English but participants might speak five or six different languages and would translate for each other and for the English-speaking facilitator. We interviewed participants over the course of their attendance (up to a year) and most – some 80% – felt that their English had significantly improved, even though the group did not overtly focus on learning English.

The by-product approach

Had the group been set up with the prime purpose of addressing issues of linguistic injustice, it might not have been quite so successful in attending to people's language needs. As with the children's art group, multilingual aims seemed to be more achievable when they were threaded through the fabric of an activity, rather than being the headline feature. Multilingual aims and outcomes can be by-products (the non-obvious intentions) of effective activities.

The by-product approach doesn't just happen by chance. Although knitting was seldom a pressing issue in these women's lives, it was a legitimate overt aim. And providing containment was one of the main functions of the group, even though it wasn't stated. Varying levels of participation were possible, depending on the participant's confidence. They could focus on a task that did not require linguistic competence. They could choose to talk or to remain silent while still being involved (via a creative activity). They could choose to take on the more empowered role of helper/producer (rather than client/consumer). And, ultimately, they could meet and make real relationships with people from the receiving community.

The activities in a 'by-product approach' can seem rather *ad hoc* and purely social rather than therapeutic. But, for this way of working to fit with a reflective clinical model, a clear rationale is needed. The proposed activity needs to be chosen because it is the optimum method of delivery for the identified outcomes/by-products. The activity here was chosen with the multilingual therapeutic frame in mind. And the final by-product of the Knitting Group exemplifies this.

After a period of time, once relationships had formed and trust was established, the group moved its meetings to a location in the town, where it was integrated into a local community art organisation and open to all. Genuine social relationships formed between residents of the receiving community and the more recent arrivals. Participants who had attended the group for between six months and six years fed back that they felt they had achieved four outcomes, some of which were therapeutic outcomes: a greater sense of belonging; a sense of being valued by the wider community; an increase in their choices of how to participate in society and, again, significant improvement in their spoken English. Fundamentally, they had a sense of their improved agency. As each group developed and moved on, a new one would be established, with a fresh group of women.

Wider systems

At the beginning of this chapter, I mentioned that groupwork could be a relevant way of attending to the role of multilingualism within a wider, international, social activist focus. The final example in this chapter is about a small-scale intervention called Colleagues Across Borders, delivered by Pásalo, the organisation that emerged as we wound down Mothertongue. This is an example of a project that attempts to address linguistic and social injustice at a far wider, global scale.

Colleagues Across Borders provides professional support and mentoring for refugees who have trained as psychosocial workers, interpreters and teachers since leaving their home countries, and who may have been affected by their traumatic experiences. The mentoring is delivered *pro bono* via Skype (and other remote platforms), by senior mental health practitioners, interpreters and teachers. The intervention is a conversation that aims to help the mentees to 'maximise their potential, develop their skills [and] improve their performance' (Parsloe & Wray, 2000: 22).

The support offered in these conversations includes information-sharing on issues ranging from models of trauma and loss to glossaries of medical terms in different languages. The support also involves listening to the mentees' own distress and frustrations and bearing witness to the sense of despair and inadequacy that accompanies such attempts to help in desperate circumstances.

Colleagues Across Borders was originally launched to provide support to refugees in their roles as psychosocial workers. However, we quickly realised that much of the psychosocial work is conducted with interpreters, and we extended the scope of the project to offer them one-to-one mentoring and training sessions.[1] The types of questions that interpreters bring to the training sessions include:

- What if the interpreter has a similar past to the client and it leads to them having an emotional reaction; how can the interpreter continue to help the client solve their situation?

- Often clients cry a lot in an interview, especially in the intake or first-time interview, and they cannot speak and explain their problem. What can I do to help them in this situation?

- What if I can't understand the accent of the Spanish and Portuguese healthcare professionals who are speaking in English. I am trying to interpret for them in my native Arabic?

- I work for an NGO that works alongside the big international charities. How can I manage this while also working and socialising in my community, who are constantly angry and frustrated with these same organisations? How can I create better barriers, remain neutral and look after myself?

- How can I suggest that someone gets psychological help without being directive?

Participants on the Colleagues Across Borders initiatives tell us that they value the content of the sessions. Equally, if not more, they value the 'by-product' of feeling accompanied across distance, nationalities and languages; they feel less isolated and that they have not been forgotten.

Conclusion

This chapter has attempted to consider the way in which multilingualism can be incorporated into the systemic frame in relation to children and young people, adults and globally, in contexts that are permeated by the challenges of linguistic justice.

---

1. For more details about the one-to-one mentoring, see Costa, Lázaro-Gutiérrez & Rausch, 2020).

I'd like to end with the words of one of the Colleagues Without Borders volunteer mentors, also from a refugee background and now living in the UK:

> I have benefitted so much from being here. I want to use these skills and do something for people from my community, who were left behind.

Even if we have not made a similar journey, we may have something to offer from within the therapeutic frame to our multilingual colleagues across the world.

References

Bialystok E, Barac R (2013). Cognitive effects. In: Grosjean F, Li P (eds). *The Psycholinguistics of Bilingualism*. Chichester: Wiley-Blackwell (pp192–213).

Buriel R, De Ment TR, Perez W, Chavez DV, Moran VR (1998). The relationship of language brokering to academic performance, biculturalism, and self-efficacy amongst Latino adolescents. *Hispanic Journal of Behavioral Sciences 20*: 283–297.

Burck C (2005). *Multilingual Living: explorations of language and subjectivity*. London: Palgrave Macmillan.

Costa B, Dioum M, Yorath S (2015). *My Languages Matter: the multilingual outlook for children in care. A White Paper*. London: Victoria Climbié Foundation.

Costa B, Lázaro-Gutiérrez R, Rausch T (2020). Self-care as an ethical responsibility: a pilot study on support provision for interpreters in human crises. *Translation and Interpreting Studies 15*(1): 36–56.

Dutt R, Phillips M (2000). Assessing black children in need and their families. In: Department of Health. *Assessing Children in Need and their Families: practice guidance*. London: Department of Health (pp37–40).

Eleftheriadou Z (2010). *Psychotherapy Across Cultures*. London: Karnac Books.

Fishman JA (1997). *In Praise of the Beloved Language: a comparative view of positive ethnolinguistic consciousness*. Berlin: Mouton de Gruyter.

Gindis B (2004). Language development in internationally adopted children. *China Connection 10*(2): 34–37.

Parsloe E, Wray M (2000). *Coaching and Mentoring: practical methods to improve learning*. London: Kogan Page.

Schmid MS (2013). First Language Attrition. *WIREs Cognitive Science 4*(2): 117–123.

Conclusion

There are many ways for models of psychological therapies to incorporate multilingual thinking. Linguistically sensitive models can help therapists and counsellors to attend compassionately to the 'second arrow' for clients, which you may remember from the Introduction: a multilingual client reminds us that the 'second arrow' comes with speaking or hearing her words in a language in which her feelings are not encoded.

You may also remember that I began the book expressing the hope that I could fulfil the aim of Pásalo and pass on some ideas and experiences about multilingualism and therapy. My intention is to encourage others to make these ideas their own and to develop them further so that health inequalities can be reduced and multilingual clients can receive the therapy services they need and deserve. Hopefully, by this stage in the book, the empty space left for multilingualism in psychological therapies now has a shape.

As Olga Tokarczuk, says: 'Anyone looking for order ought to steer clear of psychology' (2019: 17). The book is a guide, not a manual. It does not include step-by step instructions for 'doing multilingual therapy'. It does not present multilingualism in psychological therapies as a finished product. Rather, so that you don't have to start from zero and reinvent the wheel, I have presented some experiences as foundations on which future generations can create their own constructions and methods for attending to multilingualism.

The six key messages that I want to leave you with are the six themes I introduced at the beginning of the book, with brief summaries of practical ways of attending to them in therapy:

1. *The impact of people's multilingualism on the **identities** they hold in their different languages.* The practical implications for therapists include inviting clients' languages into the therapeutic space via, for example, code-switching, talking about languages, noticing how different languages are embodied differently, taking a client's language history.

2. *The **political** issue of multilingualism.* The languages we speak are a product of our world history, which includes oppressive practices. What is the legacy of those oppressive practices on the languages we speak in psychological therapies? The intergenerational implications for the languages that we use may not be readily available in people's consciousness. What happens if your own or your parents'/grandparents' original language has been suppressed or you/they were punished for speaking it? As therapists, we can help our clients to think about these issues, bring linguistic biases to light and consider the intergenerational impact of sharing and not sharing heritage languages with one's family. We can also work in a wider systemic way and respond to issues of social justice from within a multilingual therapeutic frame.

3. *The trio of **power, privilege and agency** inherent in multilingualism requires therapists to consider their own and their clients' relationships with the languages they speak.* English is often the first language of people with most power. What happens to the other tongues of our clients? In practical terms, practitioners can explore the linguistic power differential between the therapist and the client by bringing the topic into the room – talking about the talking. They can also actively consider the power dynamics from the different perspectives of the three people in the interpreter-mediated triad. Supervisors can take the initiative to bring the topic of clients' and supervisees' multilingualism into the conversation as a distinct experience worthy of consideration. Choosing to address or ignore multilingual matters in the therapeutic and supervisory relationship is an ethical issue.

4. ***Exclusion and inadequacy** are the opposite sides of the coins of privilege and agency.* These sides of the coins do not have the power to influence and create worth. It is understandable, whether you

are monolingual or multilingual, that you may feel excluded when people around you speak languages that you do not share. If you are monolingual, you can feel envious of and/or inferior to those who speak more than one language. If you are multilingual, you can assume that you are immune to these feelings, and possibly even feel superior to your monolingual colleagues. And, because of the discounted value of the currency of exclusion, it is easy to get tangled up in projections about grandiosity and victimhood. But we can try to understand the mechanisms and the political structures underlying the feelings, values and behaviours that exclusion and inadequacy evoke when we encounter multilingualism in therapy.

5. *Multilingualism is an asset in therapeutic work.* Clients can find that they express parts of themselves and their emotions differently in their different languages. They can find they connect with emotions and memories more intensely in one language or get some cognitive distance more readily in another. Clients may process trauma by using one language to approach the highly charged material safely, another language to re-experience the intensity of feelings, and can later return to the first language in order to make sense of the material and gain some mastery over their emotional reactions. The linguistic bonds (Hammer, 2016) people have with their languages are also worthy of exploration through the multilingual frame. In which languages have clients formed their attachments? How are they attached to their different languages? What has been lost and what has been gained by learning or forgetting a language? It can, understandably, seem much easier to conduct therapy in a lingua franca (English, for example). When a client speaks your first language well, you might be tempted to accept this as a technical solution to your way of working. You might leave this issue unexamined, as you might leave the air in the therapy room unexamined and excluded from the exploratory therapeutic frame. How does that impact on the therapeutic relationship?

6. *The **technical v process/relational** theme is at the heart of the multilingual therapeutic frame.* This theme provides the foundation for a theoretical and practical guide for working with the head/heart spilt, introduced at the beginning of this book in the quotation by

Nelson Mandela. Language is not a neutral communication tool (Dewaele et al, 2019). As therapists, we need to consider the technical and the relational. The technical is attractive because it offers simple solutions, but these can obscure the more complicated issues. So we need to make a commitment to engage with the relational processes that can be observed through a multilingual therapeutic filter. This commitment can take the form of remembering to think honestly about the alliances and exclusions that may be forming and how we feel about them, once the technical issues have been solved: for example, who sits where and who looks at whom in interpreter-mediated therapy. It can be a reminder to look beyond the solution and ease of working in a lingua franca, and beyond our eagerness to praise a client for their linguistic ability. Or it can be a reminder to examine our assumption that, because we too are multilingual, we understand and identify with our clients' multilingual experiences. Linguistically sensitive processes are, by their nature, also culturally sensitive processes. By exposing ourselves to situations that cause discomfort and learning how they affect us, we can aim to increase our tolerance of not understanding. And if we can allow ourselves to be a little clumsy and make cultural mistakes, we can also learn how to repair cultural injuries. Similarly, it can be useful to think about our relationships with those who hold power and how they impact on our own sense of agency. How do we react to our personal sense of powerlessness and how might that affect our work with multilingual clients or as multilingual therapists? In short, as with any therapeutic endeavour, we can try to see into those recesses where the light doesn't shine so brightly. Multilingualism has been in the dark for a long time in the study and practice of psychological therapies. If we consider multilingualism as a discreet phenomenon, we might be able to bring it out of the shadow.

And finally, I want to end as I began, with an example from my own life. Throughout our relationship, I spoke with my father in English only (other than the occasional Greek word he slipped in here and there). That was strange, for a couple of reasons. First, his English wasn't very good, and I have often wondered what might have been different in our relationship if we had shared the same language of the heart. Second, he was born in a British colony and his father, my grandfather, fought against British rule. The irony probably won't have escaped you that I wouldn't have engaged in the work I have done or written this book if I hadn't been the product of a colonial heritage.

In Kamel Daoud's novel *The Meursault Investigation*, set in Algeria, his protagonist speaks the colonial language of French, both for practical purposes and in order to express himself:

> 'You drink a language, you speak a language, and one day it owns you: and from then on, it falls into the habit of grasping things in your place, it takes over the mouth like a lover's voracious kiss. (2015: 3)

Political and personal multilingual experiences can be complex, full as they are of stories of oppression, repression, punishment, aggression, concealment, creativity and reconstruction. We may be tempted to ignore our own and others' multilingual experience because, as we have seen throughout this book, it engenders feelings of shame, envy, guilt and exclusion, among others. Discounting multilingualism, or considering it an obstacle, means we neglect a rich thread of human existence. Multilingual clients are different from monolingual clients.

The multilingual therapeutic frame can become part of our core practice. If you feel, as I do, that the time has come for the inclusion of the multilingual experience in psychological therapies, then, to paraphrase Joshua Fishman (1997), include it, and pass on what you learn to the next generation. Pass it on. It is a gift.

References

Daoud K (2015). *The Meursault Investigation*. New York: Other Press.

Dewaele J-M, Özdemir C, Karci D, Uysal S, Özdemir ED, Balta N (2019). How distinctive is the foreign language enjoyment and foreign language classroom anxiety of Kazakh learners of Turkish? [Online ahead of print.] *Applied Linguistics Review*. doi.org/10.1515/applirev-2019-0021 9 (accessed 22 June 2020).

Fishman JA (1997). *In Praise of the Beloved Language: a comparative view of positive ethnolinguistic consciousness*. Berlin: Mouton de Gruyter.

Hammer K (2016). Bilingual bonds: acculturation, attachment, and being yourself in a new language. *International Journal of Language and Culture* 3(2): 253–279.

Tokarczuk O (2019). *Flights* (J Croft, trans). London: Fitzcarraldo Editions.

Name index

A

Alexander, C 49
Amati-Mehler, J 16
Antinucci, G 40
Antonini, R 49
A Place to Belong 112–114, 115
Arab, D 62
Ayçiçegi, A 14

B

Bager-Charleson, S 69
Berko Gleason, J 14
Bernardes, D 47
Biever, JL 31
Birbeck Wellcome Trust Institutional
      Strategic Support Fund 106
Bowker, P 36
Bradford, D 52–53
Briggs, S 79
British Association for Counselling &
      Psychotherapy (BACP) 69
British Psychoanalytic Council (BPC)
      69
Bulawayo, NV 72
Burck, C 11
Byers-Heinlein, K 2

C

Caldwell-Harris, CL 14, 17
Callea, T 50
Colleagues Across Borders 118–120
Costa, A 22
Costa, B 15, 18, 19, 20, 25, 31, 79

D

Daoud, K 125
De Maesschalck, S 11
Department for Education 10
Derrida, J ix
Dewaele, J-M 1, 3, 9, 10, 18, 19, 20, 24,
      25, 26–27, 31, 33–34, 41, 70
de Zulueta, F 13, 16
Dosanijh, K 62

E

Eddo-Lodge, R 11
Eleftheriadou, Z 115
Elhabarri, S 62
Elliott, R 11
Epston, D 2

F

Fernando, S 17
Fillmore, LW 16
Fishman, J 125

G

Gardner-Chloros, P 24
Georgiadou, L 43
Get Reading 3, 10
Gilbert, P 17, 21
Gramlingm D 10
Gurung, SM 62

H

Hammer, K 16
Harris, CL 20

Hawkins, P 94
Hoffman, E 8, 9–10
Hordock, D viii

I

Imberti, P 19, 32

J

Jenson, SQ 1

K

Karpman, S 56
Kaushanskaya, M 2
Knitting Group, The 115–117
Kokaliari, E 103
Komska, Y 10

M

Mandela, N ix, 124
Marian, V 2
Maslow, AH 2
Miller, E 85
Milner, M 9
Mothertongue, vii, 2–4, 22–23, 32, 50,
        57, 61, 62, 70, 104, 116, 118
Moyd, M 10
Mungai, J 62
Muñoz, A 52–53
Muscat, M 24

N

National Health Services (NHS) 4,
        43

P

Panicacci, A 9, 19
Paquette-Smith, M 26
Pásalo Project, The 4, 62, 118, 121
Pavlenko, A 14, 19, 22
Pérez Foster, R 16, 17, 25
Phipps, A 12, 14, 27, 36
Pouyiouros, CC vii
Power, A 89, 104
Proctor, G 10

R

Richards, B 36
Rogers, CR 11
Rolland, L 18, 19, 25
Rothschild, B 9
Ryde, J 11

S

Sapir, E 12
Scarry, E 14
Schmid, MS 15, 17, 24
Schrauf, RW 20, 71
SCoPEd 69–70
Shields, G 61
Shohet, R 94
Smith, F 1
Stern, D 17
Sue, D 17
Sue, DW 17
Szekacs-Weisz, J 76

T

Tehrani, N 16, 21–23
Telvi, J 2
Tokarczuk, O 121

U

United Kingdom Council for
        Psychotherapy (UKCP) 69

V

van der Kolk, B 9, 15, 22
Van Parijs, P 10
Vaughan, S 16, 21–23
Verdinelli, S 31
Vertovec, S 10

W

White, M 2
Winnicott, DW 16

Y

Yildiz, Y 10

Subject index

A

accent 26, 33, 34, 99, 119
access
    to emotions 18, 19, 22, 35, 71, 103
    to interpretering services 27, 47, 49
    to therapy 45, 68, 74
action methods 80
additional language(s) 16, 18, 78, 114
agency
    counsellor's sense of, 124
    interpreting, 51
    linguistic, 1, 5, 11, 12, 12–16, 20, 23,
        25, 35, 72–74, 113, 122–123
    personal, 116, 118
anger, expression of 24, 35, 96
anxiety
    counsellor's, 75
    interpreter's, 82
    and multilingualism 89, 100
aphasia 74
applied linguistics 3, 14, 18
Around the Well 62
art workshops (*see* A Place to Belong)
assessment
    language, 25, 97
assumptions
    about shared language and
        experiences 40–41, 102, 124
    and unconscious bias 74–75, 104
asylum seekers 47, 59
attunement 24, 33, 41
autonomy
    client, 39

interpreter, 92–93
avoidance
    of multilingualism 36, 40–42
awareness (*see also* cultural)
    multilingual, 25, 73–74, 85, 104,
        107–108

B

back-translate 15, 24
barriers
    to communication 96
    cultural, 102
belonging
    children's sense of, 16, 113
    and identity formation 19–20
    in a new country 35, 84, 117–118
bereavement 23
Between 62
bilingual/ism 2, 17, 22
black and minority ethnic (BAME) 3
body language 2, 9, 14, 73
boundaries 38, 40, 43, 64
burnout
    interpreter, 57, 59–61, 65, 93
by-products approach 113, 117–118,
    119
bystander
    the interpreter as, 60

C

children
    as interpreters 49
    and multilingualism 114–115

clinical authority/responsibility
  of counsellor 34, 52, 54, 55, 64, 65,
    75, 80, 82, 86, 99
code of practice
  for interpreters 57–59
code-switching (*see also* language
    switching) 24, 122
cognition processes 11, 12, 15, 17,
    221
  and language 22
  and translation 103
collaboration
  prebriefing and, 83
  therapist and interpreter 52, 53–54,
    69
collaborative training 79–80,
    104–105
collective-centred 111
colloquialisms 34
collusion 41, 79
colonial
  heritage 9, 100, 125
  history 13, 26, 27
commissioners 51
compassion 21–23, 102
compensatory
  strategies 84
  techniques 74
confidentiality 6, 52, 58, 63
connectedness 14, 19, 32
containment 51, 93, 116, 117
control
  counsellor's, of sessions, 52, 55,
    95–96
  client's, 79
coping strategies
  counsellor's, 91
  defensive, 84–85
  dysfunctional, 57
core competencies 8, 68, 79, 85, 89,
    108, 125
cross-disciplinary research 3, 9, 18, 26
cross-language couples 105–107
cultural
  awareness 35, 50, 58, 70, 89, 104
  competence 69

heritage 98, 101, 114, 122
norms 49, 70

D
debrief 58, 61–62, 83
decision latitude 93, 94, 95
dialect 5, 51
dictionary
  as therapeutic tool 79, 97
drama triangle (Karpman) 56, 65,
    84–85, 96
dyad
  therapeutic 47, 54, 111, 112, 116
dynamic administration 51

E
embodiment 32, 41, 74
empathy
  linguistic, 11–12, 24–25, 35,
    72–74, 75, 77, 78, 79
encoding
  linguistic, 19, 21, 121
equity
  of access to services 47, 73, 108
ethical
  decision-making 5, 14, 70, 93
  dilemmas 39, 40
  ground rules 81
exclusion 5, 8, 57, 68, 79, 84, 107, 111,
    122–123, 124, 125
expectations
  of client 43, 100
  managers', 100

F
family
  as interpreters 49–51, 58
first language 14, 16–17, 18, 20, 41,
    73, 75–79
  attrition 15–16, 18, 76, 114
  English as, 9, 10, 11, 17, 38, 98,
    100, 122
  shared, 106–107, 123
  terminology 6, 10
  and trauma 21–24, 32, 123
fluency 15–16, 68, 116

G

gift, language as 115, 125
ground rules 58, 82–84
groupwork
  with adults 115–117
  with children (*see also Name
    index* A Place to Belong)
    112–114
  with wider systems 118–119
guilt
  and white privilege 11

H

home languages 6, 10, 14, 15, 16,
    17, 21–23, 31, 32, 40, 101,
    102–103, 112, 113
  children's, 114-115
host languages 35, 115

I

In More Words 91
In Other Words 61
inclusion 8, 57, 84, 107, 111
inequalities
  health, 9, 27, 86, 121
  power, 98
infantilisation 11, 15, 39, 72, 73, 113
insider/outsider status 111
interdependence 112
intergenerational 122
internal worlds 13, 14
intimacy 38
  of counselling dyad 47, 112, 116
isolation 115
  of interpreters 91

L

language (*see also* home languages)
  and attachment 16–17, 23–24, 76,
    123
  attrition (*see* first language)
  gap 45
  mastery 14, 112, 113
  as political issue 4, 98, 122, 123
  sign, 3, 90
  spoken, 3, 5, 14, 77

switching (*see also* code-switching)
  22, 24–25, 38, 44, 71, 122
lingua franca 6, 10
  colonial, 26
  English as, 9, 10, 17, 35, 42, 75,
    95–99
  therapy in, 23, 123, 124
linguistic
  agency 11, 12–16, 20, 25, 35, 72–74,
    113
  biases 104
  bonds 123
  capacity 1, 77
  empathy 11–12, 24, 25, 35, 71,
    72–74, 77
  history 21, 23, 25, 41
  injustice 10, 117
  loss 15, 16–17, 33, 41, 114, 115
  prestige 5, 9, 98
  privilege 10–11, 12, 26, 73, 98, 99

M

mastery
  emotional, 22, 23, 123
mentoring 118–119
meta-questions 105
migration 17, 19, 23
mini-*équipe* 54
monolingual 11, 34, 36, 43, 72, 74, 98
  comparison with multilingual
    2–3, 8
moral injury 59, 86
mother tongue 17, 22, 24, 76, 77
multilingual
  awareness 107, 108
  embodiment 1, 9, 11, 12, 32, 74,
    122
  filter 124
  identities 38, 100
  therapeutic frame 5, 9–10, 19, 21,
    24, 27, 37, 38, 40, 42, 71, 79,
    85, 89, 95, 97, 118, 120, 122,
    123, 125
  workforce 3
multilingualism
  cognitive benefits of, 115

N

native language 16, 33, 76, 78, 100, 114, 119
near-native 10
non-verbal 14, 74

P

power 1, 5, 8–9, 10–11, 26, 34, 36, 47, 48, 51, 52, 56, 63–64, 72–74, 75–79, 80–84, 122, 124
dynamics in therapy 96–99
of interpreters 92–93, 94–95
and linguistic agency 12–16
in systemtic therapy 108
prebriefing 83, 92, 95
'pseudotherapy' (Foster) 17
pulls and pushes 43, 53, 56, 65, 76

Q

'quasitherapy' (Foster) 17

R

racialisation 11
rapport 52, 56, 80
refugee 17, 22, 39, 75, 118, 119, 120
relational process 9, 24, 42, 43, 69, 71, 77, 104, 112, 123, 124
resilience and language 115
role play 86, 98, 99, 103, 105,
role reversal 36
rupture (therapeutic) 76, 104, 107

S

safeguarding 56
self-care 60
self-perception 2
shame 11, 68, 90, 98–99, 105, 125
shared language 6, 10, 40, 84, 102
simultaneous/consecutive interpreting 54
social
action/activism 112, 118
frame 38, 43, 117
injustice 118, 122
relationships 102
systems 118–119

value 102, 112
'Social Graces' (Burnham) 108
speech and language therapist 74
supervision
group,
for counsellors with multilingual clients 95–100
for multilingual counsellors and psychotherapists 100–104
for interpreters 57, 60, 90–95
linguistically sensitive, 4, 40, 42–43, 48, 89
multilingualism in, 70
training for supervisors 70, 104–108
systemic
change 93–94
preparation for interpreting 51, 53, 56, 60
therapy 108
thinking 122

T

taboo 35
tolerance
for not knowing 5, 124
training
for Colleagues Across Borders interpreters 119
multilingual, for clinical supervisors 104–109
counselling, 31, 38, 42–43, 86
experiential, 80, 104
triangular relationships 84–85
to work with interpreters 79–84
transitional space 116
transparency 55, 81, 92, 93
trauma 9, 14, 15–16, 19
role of language in recovery from 21–24, 71, 78, 123
triadic relationship 48, 52–53, 55, 56, 57, 79, 85, 122
trust (interpreter and counsellor) 53–54, 55, 58, 83

U
unconscious bias 5, 74, 75

V
values
    cultural, 50, 70
vicarious trauma (of interpreter)
        59–61, 65, 86

Psychological Therapies for Survivors of Torture:
A human-rights approach with people seeking asylum

Editor Jude Boyles
(PCCS Books, 2017)

ISBN 978 1 910919 33 0

Discounted prices and free UK postage at www.pccs-books.co.uk

This edited collection of writings by experienced therapists, social workers and interpreters working with survivors of torture in exile, fills a gap in the English-language literature with its specific focus on an increasingly important but neglected client group.

The editor, Jude Boyles, is an experienced therapist who established and managed a UK rehabilitation centre for survivors of torture in exile for 14 years. The contributors are from the voluntary and statutory sectors, and work in primary and secondary healthcare, in women's projects and in refugee therapy settings. They write from a range of psychotherapeutic perspectives and use a variety of models, but all share a holistic approach and use a human-rights framework.

Chapters cover overarching issues such as interpreter mediated therapy, assessment, and working with trauma and shame. Others explore in detail the particular needs of specific client groups such as LGBT survivors, women, separated young people, and families.

This is a book for all counsellors and therapists, but particularly those who are new to or already working with this client group. Packed with first-hand practitioner experience and survivors' stories, and written in plain English, it captures the everyday realities and challenges of survivors' lives in the UK today. This is also a book for mental health professionals and NGO workers who need a better understanding of the impact of torture and the asylum process on people's mental wellbeing.